GUSTAVUS VASA.

See page 31.

STORIES

FROM THE

HISTORY OF SWEDEN

Fredonia Books
Amsterdam, The Netherlands

Stories from the History of Sweden

by
English Society for Promoting Christian Knowledge

ISBN: 1-4101-0922-4

Copyright © 2006 by Fredonia Books

Fredonia Books
Amsterdam, The Netherlands
http://www.fredoniabooks.com

All rights reserved, including the right to reproduce this book, or portions thereof, in any form.

In order to make original editions of historical works available to scholars at an economical price, this facsimile of the original edition is reproduced from the best available copy and has been digitally enhanced to improve legibility, but the text remains unaltered to retain historical authenticity.

CONTENTS.

	PAGE
THE COPPER-MINE	7
THE SNOW KING	62
THE IRON KING	106
FALL OF THE HATS AND THE CAPS	162
PERSEVERANCE	199
THE THREE PICTURES	229

Illustrations.

	PAGE
GUSTAVUS VASA	2
GUSTAVUS ADOLPHUS	63
CHARLES THE TENTH	107
KING GUSTAVUS AND HIS OFFICERS	163
YOUNG LINNÆUS'S EARLY LESSONS IN BOTANY	198
YOUNG ERIC DECLARED KING	228

SWEDEN.

The Copper Mine.

THERE is in Sweden a province called Dalecarlia. It abounds with forests, rivers, lakes, and waterfalls. Wild and beautiful, this country does not produce much corn, and the tender bark of the pine is frequently used as a substitute by the inhabitants. The winter is very long and severe, and the summer comes so suddenly—the valleys so quickly change their snowy mantle for their green dress—that we may say there is no spring there.

> "O! 't is the touch of fairy hand,
> That wakes the spring of northern land;
> It warms not there by slow degrees
> With changeful pulse the uncertain breeze:
> But sudden on the wondering sight
> Bursts forth the beam of living light;

And instant verdure springs around,
And magic flowers bedeck the ground."

The peasants of Dalecarlia are a brave, patient race of men, who cheerfully endure both cold and hunger. They love their country, and put their trust in God. Tall in stature, hardy, independent, frank-hearted and kind, the Dalecarlians are also distinguished for their simplicity, hospitality, and piety. Industrious and prayerful, they may bow their necks as they enter their lowly dwellings, but they have never yet bowed them to the yoke of the oppressor.

It was in one of the extensive forests of Dalecarlia, the abode of the greedy wolf and savage bear, that there walked one evening, long ago,—as long since as the year 1520,—two young men, engaged in deep conversation. Though meanly clad, their noble and intellectual countenances, their high bearing, and polished manners, bespoke them to be above the rank of peasants.

"And you tell me, indeed, Olof," observed the younger of the two to his companion, "that the tyrant Dane has been crowned King of Sweden?"

"It is too true," replied Olof; "Christian of Denmark now reigns in our fatherland."

"O shame! shame!" cried young Erickson, bitterly; "where were Swedish freemen and Swedish swords, when that came to pass! Surely, surely, Olof, my countrymen did not stand tamely by and acknowledge that fierce invader as their king?"

"Alas, Erickson! the faithless tyrant, before his coronation, promised to release all prisoners, and maintain the rights and freedom of the Swedish nation. He had not been crowned three days, however, when he violated his solemn promise, by ordering the chiefs of the most respectable Swedish families, with the members of the senate, to be arrested, and then beheaded in the market-place. Eighty-four of the first men in Sweden perished on the scaffold in one day! Prepare for the worst, my dear friend; mine is a fearful tale."

"One moment, Olof, one moment," said

Erickson, in an agitated voice, "my father—my venerable father—is he ——?"

"Your father and my father, Erickson, are beyond the reach of the tyrant's power."

"Murdered? slain?" said the young noble, pale and horror-struck; "O! it cannot be! My father! my beloved father! shall I never see thee more? O, woe is me!"

The grief of the unfortunate son was extreme. His whole frame seemed shaken by the tidings of this terrible calamity, and for a time he was overwhelmed by violent sorrow. At length, with a strong effort mastering his emotion, he turned to Olof, who silently but truly sympathized with him. "Go on, Olof," he said, in a subdued voice, "I can hear all now. Go on. What said the people?"

"When they saw the wholesale murder contemplated, their horror and indignation were roused to the utmost. Restraining their feelings no longer, they rushed by thousands to the place of execution, determined, if possible, to save the noblest and best in Sweden from the headsman's ax.

Alas! it was but the signal for redoubled slaughter! Falling on the unarmed multitude, the Danish soldiers massacred all who came in their way, without distinction of age or sex. Men, women, children—none were spared. The slaughter was frightful—the streets of our capital ran with the blood of her citizens. Several hundred dead bodies lay unburied within the gates for days. I hastened from a scene so fearful, where all who were dear to me had perished."

A gloomy silence of some minutes ensued. The young nobles were brooding over their country's wrongs, and their own deep-seated griefs.

"Erickson," at length said Olof, "you have not yet told me how you escaped from the fortress where Christian had confined you. The wrath of the tyrant was extreme when he heard you had effected your freedom. I understood he laid a penalty of six thousand florins* on your jailer if he had you not in safe keeping when called for."

"Ay; Banner thought his money safe

* A florin is worth about half a dollar.

enough, and allowed me to walk and hunt in the vicinity of the fortress, little dreaming of escape. But I dreamed of it, and one fine morning, disguised as a peasant, I passed unmolested through my prison gates. A herd of cattle being on the road, I entered the service of the drover, and so escaped the notice of the men sent by Banner in pursuit of me. In safety I reached Lubec, and though my jailer tracked me thither, he in vain attempted to recapture me. The inhabitants protected me from danger, and sent me in a vessel to Sweden."

"But know you not that Christian has heard of your return, and even now seeks your life?" said Olof. "A price is set upon your head, and death is threatened to those who afford you either food or shelter."

Erickson sadly smiled. "I am safe in Dalecarlia," he said; "here they betray not the unfortunate. But the Danish tyrant fears me! Ay, and he shall fear me yet more. Hear me, Olof;—he has deprived me of father, friends, possessions;

but he has not deprived me of my will,—
he cannot crush my spirit,—and I this day
make a firm and high resolve never to
rest till my country is free! From this
hour I devote myself to Sweden. From
this hour her liberty is my great object,
and ere long, if there be any energy, any
patriotism left in the land, the Dane shall
tremble on his usurped throne."

"If her liberation can be effected, it is
you who must do it, Erickson; and who
has so good a claim as you have to be the
deliverer of our father-land? A descendant of our ancient kings, a true-hearted
Swede, who could better head her patriot
armies? Enroll me as your first follower."

"The time is not come yet, Olof; there
are numerous difficulties in the way to the
attainment of my object; but courage, patience, and perseverance will break through
them all. And now, my friend, we must
separate; it would not be safe for you to
be seen with me, and we are approaching
the village."

"Ask me not to leave you, Erickson,"
replied Olof; "we are bound by the ties

of kindred and of friendship; our country is the same, our religion the same, and from henceforth the same glorious cause will animate us both. Then with you I remain."

"No, Olof, return to Stockholm, where you can do me more service than by remaining here. You may then assist me, whereas here you would but endanger your own life."

"But you will perish, Erickson! the people will not dare to give you food or shelter; the Danish ruffians will pursue you; you will be betrayed and taken. And once more in the tyrant's power, a cruel death will be your fate!"

"My dear friend," said the young noble calmly, "I have a Protector on high. I put my trust in God. He can preserve me, and prosper the cause which I have at heart, if it be his will. Do you trust in him, also, and leave me. My faithful old servant attends me in my wanderings, and we have a sufficient supply of money for all our wants. For a time I shall be quiet, but ere long Christian shall hear of me.

Olof, seeing further expostulation useless, was obliged to acquiesce in his friend's determination, and, taking an affectionate leave of him, returned to Stockholm, while Erickson proceeded to the little village where he was at present staying.

That evening, as the young noble sat by the fire in the lowly hut, relating to his old attendant the terrible tidings he had received from Olof, the owner of the cottage, a middle-aged peasant woman, entered, and sat down by them.

"There is a little tumult in our quiet village," said she, during the first pause in the conversation; "some Danish soldiers have arrived to make search, as they say, for a rebel to the king. They have caused it to be known far and wide, that whoever gives him food or shelter shall be put to death, while, on the other hand, a large sum of money will be the reward for his capture."

"And what may be the name of this rebel to King Christian?" asked Erickson.

"Why, that is the strangest part of it," replied the woman, fixing her calm, clear eyes on the young noble,—"that is the strangest part of the story. This dangerous rebel to the Danish usurper appears to be no less a person than a brave, true-hearted Swede—a descendant of the ancient kings of Sweden—the young Gustavus Vasa! O!" she continued, as she still kept her earnest gaze on Erickson, "they made a sad mistake when they came to Dalecarlia to look for the betrayer of Gustavus Vasa. Do they think the Dalmen cowards and traitors? do they imagine them base enough to betray the unfortunate, and to refuse hospitality to the houseless stranger? Above all, is it one of the royal line of Sweden they would deliver into their cruel hands? O! they little know the peasants of Dalarna, if they think thus! Let the prince Gustavus trust himself among us, and he will find the Dalmen and Dalwomen alike faithful and loyal."

"He has trusted in you, he does trust in you," said Erickson, rising; "he knows that it is not the love of gold, or the fear of danger, that can turn the peasants of Dalecarlia from the path of honor, or cause them to forget the rights of hospitality. He has come to these mountains as to an asylum of truth and peace, and he has found in the simple mountaineers that which he has sought elsewhere in vain. To show how fully he trusts you, good Annika, he now places his life in your hands. I am Gustavus Vasa!"

"I thought it! I knew it!" said the peasant woman, as she fell on her knees before the disguised noble, and kissed his hand; "from the moment I heard the errand of the Danish soldiers I guessed it all. The first day you entered my cottage, I saw you were not the humble traveler you would have passed for; but little did I dream of your real rank. O," she continued, as the tears stood in her eyes, "it is a sad day for Sweden when the descendant of one of her ancient kings is termed a rebel!"

"It is a sad day for Sweden," said Gustavus Vasa, thoughtfully; "but the light will come yet. Sit down, good Annika, and give me your advice, for we have no time to lose. I too well know the cruel eagerness of the ferocious Danes. In another hour we may be all slaughtered. Tell me, which is the shortest path up the mountain?"

"Sir!" said Annika in surprise, "surely you are not going up the mountain?"

"I must leave you," said Gustavus, "and the mountain will be the safest hiding-place for the night. Come, Berger, prepare to march."

"But why need you leave my hut?" asked Annika.

"My good woman, have you not just heard that *death* is threatened to any one who shall shelter the rebel, Gustavus Vasa? Methinks I would not willingly bring down such a punishment on you. It would be but a poor return for your kindness and hospitality."

"And do you think, noble sir, that I would let you depart from my cottage in such a night as this, and to wander on the bleak mountain without food or shelter? No; the fear of death itself would not make me do it! I have a hiding-place, if the Danes should come, where you would be quite safe—but they will not come to-night, they are drinking too deeply. Do not hesitate, noble prince, you will be perfectly secure in this place of concealment."

"It is not for myself I hesitate, good Annika, but for you. I am used to danger, and have escaped more than once when escape seemed impossible; but you ——"

"Fear not for me, sir; I never fear when in the path of duty. I will but fasten the door a little more securely, and then prepare your supper—a poor supper for one of royal blood. I think there is a bar of iron lying outside; it will strengthen the door. I will go for it, though I trust we shall not need such a precaution."

As soon as Annika was gone, Berger approached his master. "O, sir," he said, in some agitation, "why did you let her know your name and rank? Pardon me, but it was unwise. She is now gone, doubtless, to betray you to the soldiers! Poor as she is, she must covet the gold promised for your capture."

"Out upon the thought!" replied Gustavus, indignantly. "I would as soon doubt her as I would doubt you. There is truth clearly written on her brow; and to put your suspicions to flight, here she comes, with her bar of iron in her grasp."

"I was wrong," said Berger; "but my anxiety on your account, my noble master, makes me suspicious. We shall be safe here for to-night, but to-morrow—O, how many will have an eye to the promised reward!"

"I do not think so," replied his master. "We have no reason to form such an opinion of the people of Dalecarlia. At all events, we must start to-morrow by break of day; I would not bring harm on this humble peasant for a mine of gold."

"And whither would you go, sir?"

"We will proceed westward, Berger, where we shall be in greater security. Fortunately, the purse you carry will aid us a long time yet."

There was very little conversation that evening in Annika's cottage. The good woman and her guests were alike thoughtful and sad. The fine, intelligent brow of the young Swedish noble was clouded with grief as he thought on the terrible tidings he had heard from Olof, and memory carried him back to the time when, as a happy child, he had sat on his beloved father's knee.

Annika was meditating on the events of the day, and her usually placid countenance wore an expression of anxiety as she thought of the morrow, and the danger it might bring to Gustavus Vasa. His youth, his amiable disposition and kindness of manner, had made her take a motherly interest in him from the time he first came to her dwelling, and now that interest was doubly increased. And Berger was thinking—but I will not say what he was thinking of.

When parting for the night, it was agreed that the fugitives should start at an early hour in the morning.

And very early it was when Gustavus Vasa, rising from his humble couch, first commended himself to the protection of Heaven, and then entered that part of the hut from which a rude partition divided him. He found Annika preparing the simple breakfast of the country, which consisted of barley-bread and goats'-milk. "Would that I had better to offer you, sir," said the kind-hearted woman, "and O, that it were in my power to shelter you from your enemies! Will you venture to lie concealed in my poor hut for a time? No? But what will become of you? and how will you live in this mountainous country, pursued by those merciless Danes? Alas! I tremble for your safety."

"Have no fears for me, good Annika," said Gustavus, in a cheerful tone, "I have none for myself. Berger carries for me a good sum of money, and, besides being a trusty follower, is well acquainted with your mountain passes. And shall I not find friends among the friendly Dalmen? Have I not already found a refuge from my pursuers? Have you betrayed me? No;—and whatever may be my fortunes, and whoever may be my friends, remember that it was your cottage which first sheltered, and your fidelity which first encouraged, Gustavus Vasa."

"O, sir, my hut is honored, indeed!" replied poor Annika with tears. "It will be more to me in future than a costly palace. May God protect you ever!"

"He will. I put my trust in him. But it is time we were setting forth; I must look for Berger."

The young noble had been absent only a few minutes, when he returned with a countenance somewhat troubled. "He is gone! Berger is gone!" he exclaimed, "and with him all my store. I thought I could have trusted Berger."

"Has he carried off your money, sir?" asked the astonished Annika.

"Even so. I had intrusted all to his care. For years he has been my faithful follower; but alas! what will not the love of gold do! For that he has deserted me in this moment of peril."

"O, shame! shame!" cried Annika, "and he a Swede! Better that he should go than remain with the bad thought in his heart; he might have brought you into trouble. But how will you live without money to buy food?"

"Money might have brought me into difficulty also," said Gustavus. "To find Berger untrue is far more grievous to me than the loss of any money. I must go, good Annika; he may have betrayed me from this same love of gold. Farewell! I have nothing to offer you but my gratitude."

"Farewell, sir, farewell! I shall dayly pray for your preservation."

Annika kept her word. She was a simple-hearted woman; but she had great trust in God; and when she heard how the Danish soldiers were searching the country for Gustavus Vasa, threatening with death those who should shelter him, and promising a large reward for his capture, she only prayed more earnestly that Providence would protect the unfortunate young noble. But the soldiers at length left that part of Dalecarlia, and Annika heard no more of Gustavus Vasa.

In one part of Dalecarlia stands a town which may be called *the black town.* It is generally covered with a thick smoke,—

so thick that often you cannot see three steps before you. The approach to this gloomy-looking place is by a dark and dreary road between walls and hills of brown slag. It is a town of burnt metal through which you advance; the streets are black, the houses are black, all that you see is black. No,—the water is yellow-green, and before you, where the way terminates, sulphur-colored flames ascend. The smoke has destroyed all wood and verdure; instead of grass and trees, there are deformity and desolation; and in place of the sweet smell of flowers, a constant, strong sulphureous fume. Now *you* may think this is a very disagreeable town; but the Swedes are very proud of it; indeed, it is the chief town in Dalecarlia. And as to the sulphureous smoke, though it makes one sneeze, and cough, and feel nearly suffocated at times, yet the people do not complain; and when Queen Christina visited this extraordinary place, and her courtiers expressed a fear that the strong fumes annoyed her, she answered in a cheerful tone, "God grant that such a smoke may never fail!" For this is the town of Fahlun, and it is from its large, celebrated, and valuable copper mine—which has been styled "the eighth wonder of the world"—that the smoke proceeds.

Amid all the gloom, blackness, and desolation of Fahlun, the eye rests with pleasure on two handsome churches, with their lofty towers and copper roofs; and the Christian traveler praises God for the blessed light of the glorious gospel in a place outwardly so dark and cheerless. Shall we pay a visit to this wonderful mine? As we advance along the strange and gloomy road, we hear the din of the roaring flames, and see them as they blaze wild and variably in the distance. These flames rise from the ovens where the copper is roasted. How black the streets are! and how deserted and dull! Ah! now the wind has blown the smoke right in our faces; it makes us cough terribly, but we will hasten on. There you see is the huge mouth of the great copper mine. Is it not large? What an abyss! Yes; just like a subterraneous giant opening an enormous mouth. And from this wide, deep, dark opening have been cast up for ages treasures of noble metal. God has caused the wealth of Sweden to come from the bowels of the earth and from the depths of the sea. The timber on her stately hills, the iron and copper in her mines, and the fisheries on her coasts—these are her riches. God has bestowed more, perhaps, on some other lands, but he has not forgotten Sweden; and it may be that it is the feeling of receiving all in a manner more directly from his hands, that causes the Swedes, particularly the people of Dalecarlia, to put such a simple trust in him. But no man is sent into the world to be idle; and the timber requires felling, and the mines require working, and bold and hardy fishermen must attend to the fisheries.

Now let us lean over this low fence round the mouth of the mine, and look down into the black gulf. We see nothing but a dark abyss—we hear the thunder of the blasting, and the hollow echoes repeating it. Yes, if you gaze steadfastly down, you will see a light. There is another—

and another—they move—can they be
torches carried by men? Yes; though
the men appear like birds, or rather, ants.
They are coming up from still deeper regions. It makes one giddy to look down.
You should like to *go* down, should you?
Very well. Now then, we must go into
the mine house, which stands opposite to
the descent. Here we put on a black
blouse, a leathern belt, and a felt hat with
a broad brim; this is to protect our clothes
from smoke and soot. Now we go into
the landing-room, where a fire burns which
has burnt there from time immemorial.
No one remembers when it was kindled,
and no one the day when it was put out.
Through the hundreds of years during
which the mine has been worked, this fire
has burned upon its brink. Even once
when the mine fell in, and no one could
work there, yet the miners would not allow
the fire to go out. Here are the guides
with their pine torches! We must also
each have a lighted torch. And now we
go down the dark, winding staircase.
What a wonderful place it is! we are now

two hundred and seventy feet below the surface of the earth, but you may go far, far deeper. This mine is like a subterraneous town; with its astonishing labyrinth of passages, shafts, caverns, and halls. More than twelve hundred miners were formerly employed at once in it; and it is said it would require eight days to go through all its rooms and passages. Some of these rooms have curious names. There is the Jewel, the Crown, the Scepter, Prince Oscar's Path, the Black Knight, the Imperial Apple, the North Star, the Silver Region, the King's Hall, the Copper Dragon, &c., &c. See how the walls glitter when the guide strikes his torch against them! Look at the beautiful colors, red, gold, and green. When the great Gustavus Adolphus stood in one of these rooms, where the bright copper ore shone from walls, floor, and roof, he exclaimed, "Where is the monarch who has such a palace as that in which we now are!"

Almost all the kings and queens of Sweden have visited this mine. Charles the Ninth called it "Sweden's Fortune," and desired that the great room might be named "The Room of God's Gifts." The poor miners have not a pleasant life, but they are contented. It is cold, damp, gloomy, and always night in the mine. And dangerous too! there are many places where, if your foot slipped,—and the ground is very slippery,—you would fall down into a black gulf! And sometimes part of the mine falls in, and buries the poor workmen alive, or crushes them to death. But they know *who* can protect them; and every Sunday, after the sermon is concluded, the clergyman offers up the following prayer in the church:—

"We thank thee, merciful God, for the rich treasures and abundant blessings which thou hast graciously conferred on this place, out of the bowels of the earth, and out of the flinty rocks; and we pray thee, that thou wilt continue to give, to bless, and to preserve to us these precious treasures; and give us grace to use these thy blessings with thankfulness, and to the honor of thy name. Preserve, O God, all those who labor in the deep and perilous regions of the earth from injury, and danger, and all evil, and give them grace to keep thee perpetually before their eyes; to commit themselves, body and soul, into thy hands; to consider always the dangers which hang over them, and thus be well prepared, should any violence befall them, to depart hence in blessedness, through thy Son, Jesus Christ our Lord. Amen."

For centuries has this prayer been used in the mining districts of Dalecarlia.

It was at the mouth of the great copper mine of Fahlun that a man stood one day, long ago, looking down into the black abyss.* His clothes were ragged, and his countenance pale and wan; but he seemed insensible to hunger and fatigue, as he gazed with wonder, curiosity, and admiration into the subterraneous world below. Long he gazed, and busy were his thoughts, till at length rousing himself, he exclaimed, "Yes! He who can make the earth thus yield her hidden treasures, can supply the wants of all his creatures. Shame on

* See Frontispiece.

me, that for a moment I doubted his fatherly care. My trust in him is strengthened. He will preserve me in the deep mine, as he has preserved me on the mountain-top. I will at once engage myself as a miner."

And it was not long before he was working in the mine, first having been supplied with food, of which he had tasted none for two days.

Do you wish to know the name of the man who thus put his trust in a watchful Providence? It was Gustavus Vasa.

Through many dangers and difficulties he had reached Fahlun. Forlorn, destitute, and half-starved, he determined to lie concealed in the mines till the search after him was a little abated. But adverse as his circumstances were, the hopes he entertained of one day effecting the deliverance of his country did not forsake him; down in the deep, dark mine, toiling like a slave for his dayly bread, Gustavus Vasa was still—as he had ever been—hopeful, trustful, resolute.

Though it was not a pleasant life—to be

shut out from the pure light of heaven, a hundred and twenty fathoms deep in the hard, cold, damp, dark, glittering mine; to see continually the same black vaulted passages, and empty halls and excavations, which seemed to have no end; always to feel the same damp air, and perpetual drippings from the roof; to meet constantly the same black figures with their solemn, pale, grimy countenances, and slow heavy steps; to know the danger, if by some accident the torch should go out, of being lost in the labyrinth of passages, or falling headlong into a fearful chasm;—this was anything but a pleasant life. But the young nobleman bore it cheerfully, and though associating with companions so far inferior in birth and station to himself, he did not on that account disdain them. On the contrary, he endeavored to lighten their labor by teaching them the following song, which still often sounds, both by night and day, in the depths of the copper mine:—

"Up, brothers! let your torches glow!
Where duty calls us let us go;

Our way, though dark, is light to keep,
   Though down into the deep.

"No matter though our path lies through
The yawning shaft, our watch is true;
No matter though that path be long,
   The longer is our song.

"The mountain opens as we go,
With gladsome hopes we march below,
Hoping a better world to find
   Than that we leave behind.

"That better world is all our own,
Its wealth transcends all treasures known,
A thousand years has flow'd its ore,
   And shall a thousand more.

"The world above is great and sheen,
But here the mine itself is green,
And in itself a wealth doth hold
   Exhaustless, and untold.

"Such joy the earth cannot impart
As when we see the copper start,
'Mid smoke and dust behold it shine,
   Forth bursting from the mine."

And he talked to them, whenever an opportunity occcurred, on the subject which lay nearest his heart, the freedom of his native land. He spoke of the frightful massacre at Stockholm, and of the unheard-of cruelties of the Danish tyrant.

THE COPPER MINE.

He told them of his hanging the peasants for the slightest offenses, of his beheading the nobles for no offense at all; how he had inhumanly caused two little boys of the ages of seven and nine to be whipped to death, and how he had barbarously ordered several Swedish ladies of rank to be thrown into the sea, after having first compelled them to make the sacks in which they were to be put! These monstrous cruelties, which gained for King Christian the title of "the Nero of the North," were listened to by the miners with abhorrence. They felt the yoke under which their country groaned, and earnestly desired to have a share in her deliverance. And when they spoke their wishes to Gustavus Vasa, and asked what could be done for Sweden, he would tell them the time was not come *yet*, but ere long their country would ask their help. Then turning to them with a look of calm confidence, he would say, "In the mean time this can you do—

> Thou Swede, put firmly thy trust in God,
> And ardently call thou upon him."

The superior mind of Gustaf, as he was called, the graces of his person and conversation, and his refined and winning manners, soon began to be talked about among his fellow-laborers. They began to think he must be above the rank of a peasant, and their suspicions were further increased by a circumstance which occurred not very long after he had entered the mines. It happened that one of the miners met with an accident, and Gustavus, who was working near, in hastening to assist him, struck his head rather severely against a sharp point of a projecting rock. He thought not of himself, however, till he had attended to his companion, when, having conveyed him to a part of the mine where his wound could be dressed, he found that his own head was streaming with blood. Smilingly observing that "it made more show than pain," he applied a simple remedy to the wound, and was soon singing cheerfully at his work again.

"That is a noble fellow!" said one miner to another as he left them; "how kindly and tenderly he cared for poor

Steen, yet he thinks nothing of his own hurt, though it is not a trifling one."

"He is noble in more respects than one, friend Behn, or I am much mistaken. Did you notice, when he took the handkerchief off his neck, how finely the collar of his shirt was worked—embroidered, I think they call it? Depend upon it, friend, Gustaf is not what he appears to be; that black dress and begrimed face are as little suited to him, as a king's cloak would be to me."

"Dost think so?" replied Behn; "well, I have had the same thoughts myself before this; he *is* different from all of us. However, noble or not, there is not in the mine a braver or kinder heart than Gustaf's."

"Most true, Behn, we all feel that; but Gustaf was not born to be a miner."

The story of the embroidered collar was talked of. It excited the curiosity of the miners, and at length they agreed among themselves that their friend Gustaf must be some person of rank in disguise, who had been forced by the tyranny of the government to take shelter in these remote parts. In a little time a neighboring gentleman heard of the circumstance. Partly from curiosity and partly from compassion, he visited the mine. Gustaf, unconscious that he had excited any particular notice, was diligently laboring, while his manly voice might be heard above his companions' as from many hundred feet deep in the earth, their song arose:—

"Up, brothers! let your torches glow!"

The moment the gentleman fixed his eyes on Gustaf, who was pointed out to him, his astonishment was extreme, to recognize in the noble features of the black miner his friend Gustavus Vasa, whose acquaintance he had made at the university of Upsal! Touched with deep compassion at the deplorable situation of so distinguished a nobleman, he could scarcely refrain from tears, but, however, had presence of mind enough not to make the discovery. Hastily writing a few lines, which he desired might be given to Gustaf, he left the copper mine, pondering on what he had seen. At night, when Gustavus went to him, he received him with great kindness, made him an offer of his house, and gave him the strongest assurances of his friendship and protection.

"My dear Gustavus," he said, "I grieve indeed to see you thus; throw off this dress, which ill becomes *you*, and come to my house. You will find better accommodation here than in the mines, and, I give you my word, equal security. Should there even be a chance of discovery, I, with all my friends and vassals, will take arms in your defense."

This offer was received with joy by Gustavus. He took leave of the mines, and for some time remained in his friend's house. But the thoughts of the young patriot ever turned on one subject; it was not a life of security and ease which could divert his mind from his country's sorrows. In vain, however, did he endeavor to induce his kind host to take part in his designs for her deliverance; arguments and entreaties were alike useless.

"I grieve for my country, Gustavus," he would say, "deeply grieve; but what can I do? It is not a handful of men that can put down the Danish tyrant. He is too strong for us. We must wait patiently; better days may come. Were we to attempt a rising now, it would only be the signal for more cruelties."

"And is not the land full of his cruelties already?" Gustavus replied. "Is not our country *groaning* under the Danish yoke? O, my friend, a few bold hearts, united in the same glorious cause, might soon strike a decisive blow for Sweden and liberty. The race is not always given to the swift, nor the battle to the strong. In defense of our country, our religion, and our homes, I entreat you to join with me."

All was of no avail, and Gustavus Vasa, with a sorrowing heart, perceived it. But he could no longer remain idle, and quitting his friend, went to the house of a gentleman named Peterson, whom he had formerly known, and who lived at a little distance.

Peterson knew him at once, and receiving him kindly and even respectfully, as the descendant of a royal line, bade him welcome to his house. On hearing the wishes and plans of Gustavus, he entered with apparent eagerness into them.

"I will raise my vassals at once," he said; "who would be backward in the sacred cause of liberty! Yes, truly and heartily I join you, sir; you may command me, my wealth, my friends, my vassals. You will soon find Swedes who love their land well enough to fight for her freedom, and who will gladly follow you as their leader. I will put down for you the names of several who, I know, will join heart and hand in the cause."

All this promised well, and with a grateful heart Gustavus warmly thanked his friend. His hopes were raised, his spirits cheered, and his eyes sparkled with animation as he read the list which Peterson put into his hands.

"This is good!" he exclaimed; "this gives hope! Sweden will yet be free; her sons will yet live in peace and security. O! Peterson, with a few more such as you we should soon force the Danes back into their own land."

The young nobleman remained for two or three days in Peterson's house, and by his amiable manners and kind disposition won the esteem and affection of all the inmates. The children became very fond of him; for when not engaged in business with their father, he was quite ready to join in their games, and be the merriest of the merry. He would answer all their questions, and tell them stories which at once delighted and interested them.

One evening as he was thus engaged with the children, their mother beckoned him from the room. "Do you remain here," she said to the little ones, who were hurrying after him; "Gustavus is going to hide, and then you shall look for him."

This satisfied the children, who shut the door and began to guess all the likely places in which their friend would hide. In the mean time their mother, a true Dalwoman, took her guest to a window. "Look there," she said, "look among the trees—what do you see?"

"A soldier! a Danish soldier!" replied

Gustavus, starting; "and more than one—there are several; I am betrayed!"

"There are a score of horsemen surrounding the house, sir; if you would escape, you have not a moment to lose."

"But who can have betrayed me?" asked the young noble, fixing his eyes on her. "Could it be Peterson?"

"Ask me not, sir, ask me not," said Peterson's wife in a hurried manner; "enough that if one has betrayed you, I am ready to assist in your escape. You have been too kind to my children to let me see you a prisoner without an attempt for your safety. Come this way, if you value your life."

She hurried him along several passages to an outhouse in the yard. "Now put on this laborer's frock," she said, "and tie this handkerchief round your head. That is right; you are well disguised. Go out through the gate, by the fir-trees, and take the path to your left; it leads you through the wood. Should any one meet you, walk slowly and lean on this stick; they will take you for the poor sick lad who comes here for milk. Now go; every moment is precious. Farewell! and God be with you!"

With hasty but sincere thanks, Gustavus departed. It was high time. The gate had scarcely closed upon him, when several horsemen rode at full speed into the yard. They were headed by Peterson himself, who, smiling exultingly as he dismounted, exclaimed, "I do not think you will be mistaken this time, gentlemen!"

"No, we have him at last," replied the soldiers; "King Christian will not forget you for this day's good work, friend Peterson."

When the treacherous host went to the sitting-room, and inquired for Gustavus, the children all declared he was hiding; but that they would soon find out his place of concealment. And while they searched through the various rooms and passages of the old house, Peterson went to the soldiers, and desired them to keep a strict watch that no one left it. "We have him!" he said to the officer in command; "he is playing at hide-and-seek with the children; it is a game he has played in earnest before now."

In the mean time, Gustavus Vasa pursued his way through the wood. Night came on, but he dared not seek refuge in any hut so near Peterson's abode. It was winter, and the cold was intense; a less hardy frame than his could scarcely have endured it. The young nobleman, however, bore it well; perhaps the thoughts which crowded into his mind, made him, in a measure, insensible to bodily pain. These thoughts were, for a time, desponding ones; but a glance at the starry firmament above him restored his mind to its usual state of calm, trustful confidence in God. Again his resolute spirit rose to meet adversity; again, as he thought on his past preservations, he hoped for the future.

And truly he had need of resolution. It required indeed a mind of no common character, a spirit not easily daunted, to meet undismayed the dangers and difficulties which crowded on his path. Again a fugitive and a wanderer in his native land;

pursued by the relentless Danes; often in want of food, and afraid to ask for shelter, he suffered, in the middle of a hard winter, hardships and privations of which you, dear children, have no conception. At one time, he had scarcely a moment to conceal himself under a fallen fir-tree, before a party of Danish soldiers galloped up; at another time he was obliged to hide in a ditch; and once he was so exhausted from cold, hunger, and fatigue, that some peasants found him nearly frozen to death in a wood. They took him to the house of a farmer, named Ferhson, who paid him every attention, and where, happily, he was restored to health. Seeing him in the garb of a peasant, the farmer asked him if he would engage as a laborer with him. Gustavus gladly assented, and at once entered on his duties as a farm-servant. Here he soon became a favorite with master and men. He was so active, strong, and industrious, and so quick and clever in his work,—just as diligent, whether his master's eye was upon him or not,—that it was not long before Ferhson found he had acquired a most valuable servant. And he was so good-natured and cheerful, so ready to give his help to others, and had so much to tell, as in an evening they clustered round the wood fire, that the laborers all agreed in declaring Gustaf to be the best companion who had come among them for many a long day. The conversation of the noble Gustavus, though varied, generally turned on the subject which ever occupied his thoughts. And eagerly the simple Dalmen listened, as he spoke, with his eloquent tongue, of the blessings of freedom; and truly did their hearts respond to his ardent wishes for Sweden's deliverance. With scarcely less interest they heard him speak of the great conflict of religious opinions then going on in Germany; of the celebrated Martin Luther, standing up to resist the Pope and his edicts; of the errors of the Romish Church, and the beauty, simplicity, and grandeur of the Protestant faith; "a faith," said Gustavus Vasa, "which I trust will be the faith of Sweden; it is already widely spreading in our land; yes,—I look forward with hope to seeing our country a truly Protestant country."

One day, when Gustavus had been some weeks at the farm, Ferhson sent for him. "I wish to speak with you, young man," said the farmer, carefully closing the door, as Gustavus entered the room. "Last night, unobserved by any, I was a listener to your conversation with my laborers. I was, I confess, astonished at what I heard. For some reason you are in disguise. Your eloquence, your information, the very tone of your voice, and step, all convince me that you are no peasant. But to me you have been a faithful servant, and to you I will be a faithful friend. Tell me how I can assist you, and I will do so to the utmost of my power."

The young noble stood for a few moments in a thoughtful attitude, his eyes fixed on the ground, then raising them with their usual calm expression, he said, "I can trust you, Ferhson—I am Gustavus Vasa!"

"Gustavus Vasa!" exclaimed the astonished farmer; "is it possible? Can it be?

It is! it is! blind that I was not to see it before! I thought last evening it might be one of our persecuted nobles to whose discourse I listened with so much pleasure; but little did I dream of discovering in this disguise the descendant of Sweden's kings, the patrotic Gustavus Vasa! Noble sir, what can I do for you?"

"Let me be your servant still, Ferhson; it will be but for a short time longer."

"A servant! no, that cannot be; you must remain in this house as its honored guest. Are not you, of all Sweden's sons, the one who most truly seeks her welfare? Do not many hearts, in despair, turn to you as the only hope for our unhappy land? Have not even my children wept as they heard the tale of your unparalleled misfortunes? Remain in this house, as its master, noble prince, for here your name is loved and honored."

"If I am to be master," said Gustavus, smiling, "I must be obeyed. It will be safer for both, Ferhson, that for the present I wear this disguise, and continue to labor as I have done."

It required some persuasion to induce the honest farmer to agree to this plan; but the event proved Gustavus to be right in his caution. Only two mornings after this discovery on the part of Ferhson, as Gustavus was laboring at some distance from him, a party of Danish soldiers rode up to the farm-house, and commenced a search for the rebel, Gustavus Vasa! Ferhson, though much alarmed, had the presence of mind to call his little son, and say to him, "Run, child, as fast as you can run, to the barn on the further side of the pond, and tell the laborers who are threshing there, Gustaf and Peter, that a party of fine soldiers have come, and they must be quick if they want to see the grand sight. Now show me how fast you can run, there's a brave boy."

The hardy little fellow soon delivered his message, and Gustavus, taking the timely hint, instantly prepared once more to flee —he knew not whither. But his fellow-laborer, Peter Nilson, seeing that there was something to alarm Gustaf in the child's words, directed him to his hut in the wood, "where," he said in a whisper, "you will be quite safe from the cruel Danes, friend Gustaf, if, as I suspect, it is you they seek."

Gustavus saw the truth written on the Dalman's brow, and fled to his cottage. The next morning, Nilson concealed him in a cart, under a load of straw, and conveyed him to Rattvik. Ferhson, knowing he could trust Nilson, had desired him to do so, and the peasant gladly obeyed; for the regard he bore Gustaf was now mingled with compassion and respect. As he walked by the side of the cart, taking care that the fugitive should have some air, they were overtaken by the soldiers, who, having passed the night at the farm, were now returning full of fury at their fresh disappointment. "Stop the cart!" they shouted to Nilson, as they rode up; "that load of straw may conceal the rebel we seek; at all events we will make sure. He shall not escape us again."

Poor Nilson was obliged to obey, and you may imagine what he felt when he saw the cruel soldiers surround the cart, and rudely thrust their sharp pikes into the straw! "If he *is* here, this will bring him out!" they cried; and, alas! Gustavus received a deep wound in his side as they spoke. The pain was great, but he endured it without a groan, and the soldiers, satisfied that he could not be there, rode on, though not without bestowing on Nilson a hearty blow. Much alarmed for the safety of the fugitive, the peasant anxiously inquired how he fared. "I have been hurt," said Gustavus; "but drive on, good Nilson." Nilson did so, and on their arrival in Rattvik carefully attended to the wound, from which the blood flowed freely.

Gustavus had scarcely recoverd from the fever which his pain brought on, than with renewed ardor he went from hut to hut, exhorting the people to throw off the Danish yoke. They listened to what he said with eagerness; his ready eloquence and graceful address quite won the hearts of these simple mountaineers. But his adventures were not over.

"As the river Dalelf runs through Dalarna, so runs the life-pulse of religion through the laborious existence of the Dal people." And a peasant woman sat spinning at the door of her hut; and poor, but contented, calm, and grateful for the blessings she enjoyed, sang as she spun:—

"God strengthen and gladden the people who dwell
By river, on hill, and in Dalom."

Before her lay the silvery Silja Lake— the eye of Dalarna—clear as a mirror; around her were the blue hills, a constant line of beauty in the landscape; here were the dark pine woods with their red, delicate flowers; and there, fields of young rye, trembling in the evening breeze. It was the glad season of nature's awakening from the long sleep of winter, and the eyes of Larsson's wife glistened with joy as she contemplated the beauteous scene. But suddenly her look becomes troubled. What does she see in the distance? What can it be which makes her spinning cease, and which causes her cheek to grow pale? Ah! she sees the Danish soldiers! she fears by their haste that they are on some errand of cruelty. She knows that Gustavus Vasa is in the neighborhood; she has heard of his misfortunes; she deeply pities the persecuted noble, and she fears he is in danger. And see! they come nearer—their swords glistening in the sun, as they spur their horses on by the side of the crystal lake. "Alas! what can they want?" said the Dalwoman, as she tremblingly gazed; "their haste bodes no good; I fear they are in pursuit of some one."

"They are in pursuit of me," said a voice by her side; "will you give me shelter? I am Gustavus Vasa."

"Gustavus Vasa!" exclaimed the astonished peasant. For a moment she was lost in surprise, but it was but for a moment. "Come this way, sir," she said; "if I *can* save you, I will."

She hurried him into her cottage, and down some steep, broken stone steps into a dark cellar. "I trust you will escape them this time," she said; "but I will take a further precaution," and ascending the steps, she firmly secured the trap-door through which they had entered, and then turned a great brewing-tub over it, so that it was not seen.

Scarcely had she sat down to her spinning-wheel, when the soldiers appeared.

"We will search every cottage," said the officer in command; "perhaps we may find him in this one; I am convinced he is lurking near." They entered; and Larsson's wife, calmly rising from her spinning, said, "You are welcome to search in my poor hut, sirs; it is not much you will find there." After looking into the two rooms and opening the cupboard doors, a soldier said in a low voice to his commander, "He cannot be here; the woman would never be so calm."

"Tell me," said the officer to the Dalwoman, "if a fugitive rebel, like Gustavus Vasa, came to you for shelter, would you admit him?"

"I have never yet turned any one from my door, or refused hospitality to a stranger," replied the peasant, calmly, "and that reminds me I have not offered you a cup of my last brewing. Let me do so now." The officer took the proffered draught, and then departed; calling out, as he galloped off with his party, "Remember! if I find you ever extend your hospitality to Gustavus Vasa, nothing shall save you from instant death!"

The Dalwoman watched them till out of sight, and then hastened to call the noble fugitive from his hiding-place, and to set before him the best food she could provide. He thanked her for her fidelity and courage, and spoke to her of his designs for Sweden's deliverance, till her heart grew glad at the thought. And good Larsson's heart was glad too when he returned home, and heard what had happened; and many conversations took place, and many plans were laid in that cottage, on the subject of Sweden's welfare.

But again the Danes forced the patriot from his kindly shelter, and once more he fled through the solitary forests, and over the pine-clad mountains. By night sleeping in the lonely sheds erected for the poor wayfarer, he followed the Dalelf through the boundless and snow-filled woods. More and more desolate became the country, and wilder rushed the rivers, while Gustavus Vasa pursued his solitary course. Did he not despair now? No; as he climbed those mountains, his hopes, his energy, his undaunted resolution, his trust in God, were all strong as ever. And then came after him, through the woods, the swift snow-skaters, to persuade him to return, and put himself at the head of the peasantry by the Silja Lake, who, roused by Danish cruelty, were only desirous to throw off the Danish yoke. O that was a joyful message for Gustavus! With a heart full of high hopes and glad resolves, he returned—to accomplish that which he had so long desired—the assembling of the peasantry of Sweden to the battle for Sweden's deliverance. Now the hour so long waited for—so long hoped for—was come; now, the light was beginning to break!

It was on a feast day, as the men of Mora came out of church, that Gustavus Vasa first addressed them. He stood on a little eminence, and eloquently did he describe the miseries of Sweden, as the peasants gathered round him, contemplating attentively the young and noble patriot, of whose unmerited persecutions they had heard so much.

"He has a manly voice, and a winning tongue," said one old man; "and see, the north wind blows—a good omen—let us attend to what he says."

Well they listened, and well he spoke. Every word of that address, so full of truth and eloquence, sunk deep into the hearts of the men of Mora. After touchingly describing the wretchedness of their beloved country under the oppressive yoke of the Danes, and the blessings of freedom, Gustavus concluded in these words:—"You, Dalmen, have at all times been brave and undaunted when the weal of your country was concerned, and therefore are you renowned in our chronicles, and all the inhabitants of Sweden turn now their eyes upon you; for they are accustomed to look on you as the firm defense and protection of our native land.

"Gladly will I join you, and will for

you spare neither my hand nor my blood; for more the tyrant has not left me. And then shall he understand that Swedish men are faithful and brave, and that they may be governed by law, but not by the yoke."

"He shall! he shall!" shouted the Dalmen, with one voice; "we will rise for Sweden and liberty! Do you lead us on, noble Lord Gustavus; the Dalmen will be your followers and your body-guard in life and in death. Yes; our mountain homes shall be as free as the mountain breeze?"

And where do you think Gustavus Vasa first marched with his four hundred Mora men? To the copper-mine at Fahlun. It was there, aided by the hardy miners, that he gained the first victory over his enemies, that he first raised the banner of his country's freedom. It was from the copper-mine in which he had labored that he began that career of victory which did not cease till the liberty of Sweden was accomplished, and himself, by the free choice of a grateful people, elevated to its throne. For, from Fahlun his strength increased with every step, the patriot Swedes gathered around him, and he soon found himself at the head of 15,000 men. One town after another fell into his hands, and, at last, Stockholm itself. The tyrant Christian was obliged to retire into Denmark, and then his country, with gratitude and enthusiasm, offered the crown to Gustavus Vasa. He refused it, but took the title of Stadtholder. Peace and security from the Danes, however, could not be obtained as long as the throne of Sweden remained vacant, and at length, to the universal joy of the people, Gustavus was crowned king. This was in 1527. He established Protestantism in Sweden, and reigned thirty-three years. During this long period he displayed such virtues and such talents for government, that he acquired fresh and imperishable claims on the gratitude of his country, and his memory is, to this day, cherished by every Swede.

Now, dear children, if ever you are inclined to be daunted by difficulties, or cast down by troubles and disappointments, remember Gustavus Vasa. Think of his patience, his perseverance, and his trust in God; and ask yourselves if your trouble is as great as his, when, toiling like a slave, he was down a hundred fathoms deep, in the dark gloomy copper-mine.

The Snow-King.

About two hundred years ago, there was assembled in the castle of Arnheim, near Stockholm, a happy Christmas party. General Arnheim, who loved to see merry faces around him at that joyous season, had collected all his children and grandchildren under the paternal roof. And a cheerful sight it was to witness the sports and glee of the youthful troop; and pleasant it was to hear the merry peals of laughter which resounded through the old castle of Arnheim. The general thought so; his eye always grew brighter at such times.

One of the greatest treats to these gladsome children was, when sitting in the evening round the large blazing wood fire in the great hall, they could prevail on their grandpapa to talk to them of former days, or tell them some wondrous story. For he had fought under the banners of

GUSTAVUS ADOLPHUS.

See page 71.

the great Gustavus Adolphus, "the Lion of the North, and Bulwark of the Protestant Faith;" he had been in many distant lands, and seen many strange sights; and he had such a pleasant way of relating the different scenes in his eventful life, and the anecdotes with which his mind was stored! and he was so kind too! But he enforced strict and prompt obedience from all, even from the very youngest; and the children, well brought up, rarely disputed the will of those whom they were early taught to obey.

One evening, when thus assembled, after a day of great enjoyment, Eric, a fine boy of ten years of age, exclaimed, " O, grandpapa! we had such fine games on the lake to-day! and we met an old soldier, who came across the Baltic in his sledge last week. It is frozen very hard indeed this winter; and he met with so many adventures—once he was nearly buried in a snow-drift, and once he lost his way. How I should like to have been with him!"

"And he told us, grandpapa," said the little Eva, "that in some countries there is no ice. How very strange that must be!"

"But," continued Eric, "he had fought in 'the Thirty Years' War,' and was severely wounded at the battle of Leipsic. I stayed talking to him till it was nearly dark; and now, dear grandpapa, will you tell me how it was that King Gustavus was so beloved by his soldiers? That old man's eyes were full of tears as he spoke of him, though it is nearly thirty years since he died at Lutzen."

"No wonder, my boy, no wonder," replied the general. "Gustavus Adolphus endeared himself to all classes of his subjects, but by his army he was loved in no common degree. His commanding intellect and unrivaled military talents caused us to place unbounded confidence in him; while his bravery, humanity, justice, and piety, won our esteem and love. A great king and an able general, he was equally distinguished for the virtues which adorn and dignify life. He was a pious Christian, a sincere friend, a tender husband, a dutiful son, and an affectionate parent.

We may truly say that Gustavus Adolphus was one of the greatest princes that ever swayed a scepter."

"He kept up great discipline in his army, did he not?" said Frederic.

"He did indeed. From the highest general to the meanest horse-boy, no one dared to disobey; yet each and all were ready to lay down their lives for him. No gaming or expensive luxuries were permitted in his camp; the officers were not allowed to indulge in dress or show; the men were taught moderation and frugality. All outrages, especially theft, dueling, gambling, and impiety, were punished with rigid severity. On taking a town, or in marching through an enemy's country, all pillage and cruelty were strictly forbidden. The king himself was a bright example of that which he enjoined on others. No gold or silver glittered in his tent; he disdained not the humble fare of the private soldier;—religion was the guide of his life. He was at once the legislator, and the most scrupulous observer of the law."

"And as to his bravery, grandpapa, the day when, sword in hand, he fell on the plains of Lutzen affords sufficient proof of that."

"Ah! that day was a sad one for Sweden. She lost at one blow her king, her general, her father, and her friend!"

"You were in that battle, grandpapa," said Ulrica; "were you near the king when he fell?"

"No, my child, I was not. The first intimation I had of the sad event was seeing his riderless and blood-stained steed galloping through the ranks. The dismal tidings thus announced to the troops, a wild cry arose of 'The king is slain! the king is slain!' There was no need then to encourage and lead on the men. The fate of their beloved monarch inspired them with redoubled energy. Their courage was excited almost to madness, and pressing on to revenge his fall, the terrors of danger and death were alike disregarded. Like enraged lions they rushed on the Austrians. The battle continued nine hours after the death of the king, and terminated in the defeat of the Austrians; but we could not rejoice in our victory, it was too dearly bought."

"Was not the king galloping forward to rally some troops when the fatal shot was fired?" asked Olga.

"Yes, my love. The intrepid hero had been wounded in the arm, and, though faint and bleeding, was endeavoring to conceal it from the soldiers, when a second shot laid him low. Then arose a desperate and fearful contest! But a shower of balls dispersed or killed those who rushed to the aid of their beloved monarch, and Gustavus expired, his last words being, 'Alas! my poor queen! my poor queen!' Two of his faithful officers threw themselves across his body, and breathed their last in defense of it. In protecting the dear and honored remains from the enemy, numbers were slain. The Yellow Guard of Gustavus—his favorite band—was cut to pieces, and lay on the ground close by the spot where he had fallen, precisely in the order in which they had met the foe, having disdained to yield one inch. Yes, the love of our soldiers to their king was fully proved at the eventful battle of Lutzen."

"But was he not buried at Stockholm?" asked Theodore.

"He was, amid the tears of a nation. He was only thirty-eight when he died."

"When did you last see him, grandpapa?"

"Just before the battle I had been conversing with him, and was struck with his calm composure as he gave me some orders. His manner was more than usually kind and winning. 'We know not what may be the event of this contest,' he said, 'but it will be a severe one. Wallenstein is not one to give way. We must trust in God for victory, general; he orders all things well.'

"As he rode along the lines, after the usual divine service, he addressed the men, saying, 'My companions and friends, acquit yourselves like men of service today. Observe your orders, and behave valiantly, for your own sakes as well as mine. I will lead you on.' An universal and enthusiastic shout from the army expressed the determination of the soldiers to follow wherever he led."

"Did he always have prayers before a battle?" said Ulrica.

"Always. He used to say 'a good Christian could not make a bad soldier,' and he himself was a bright example to his army of piety and trust in God. He was in the habit of constantly reading the Holy Scriptures; several times, on entering his tent, have I found him engaged in the perusal of the sacred volume, when we thought he was occupied with plans of battles or sieges."

"But why did King Gustavus go to battle, then, dear grandpapa? for the Bible tells us to live in peace with one another."

"War is a sad thing, Eva, and Gustavus knew its horrors. But the oppressed Protestants of Germany had loudly called to him for help. He was firm in his attachment to the Protestant faith; they were persecuted and groaning under the tyranny of Austria, and he stood forward as their deliverer."

"Do you think the time will ever come when there will be no more fighting in the world?" asked little Eva.

"Our Bible tells us there will be such a time, my child. But people must cease to be selfish, and covetous, and cruel, before that day can be. Our good king did what he could to alleviate the horrors of war; but still, wherever war is, there must be misery, and desolation, and death."

"Well, for my part," said Eric, "I should like to have gone with the great Gustavus to battle, if it were but to *see* the fight."

"Ah! my boy, you would soon have seen enough, when you had walked over the battle-field after a victory. But I remember two brothers, fine boys about your own age, who had the same desire as you have, and who *were* in the camp of Gustavus Adolphus;—shall I tell you of their fate?"

"O! pray do."

"You must know, then, that our beloved monarch always endeavored to teach his soldiers moderation and humanity. Wherever we were, and on whatever service employed, the public worship of God formed one of our most important duties; for, to be taught our duty to God was, the king well knew, the surest and truest way of learning our duty to our neighbor. Every regiment had two chaplains, who were generally respected and beloved by the soldiers. At dawn of day, each regiment, assembled by beat of drum, formed a circle around the chaplain appointed to attend it. Suitable prayers were offered up, and a psalm or hymn chanted by all present; after which, the minister delivered a short sermon. The boys were then sent to school, which was regularly opened in a particular part of the camp reserved for the purpose. If there were no important duties to be performed, every one betook himself to some useful occupation. The greatest order and regularity prevailed throughout the army, swearing and all gambling, as I said, being strictly forbidden. At sunset, the roll of the drum again summoned us to prayer; and after the watch was set, we tranquilly went to rest, feeling that the Almighty, whose protection we had implored, would defend us from harm and danger."

"But how did the soldiers employ themselves all day, when there was no fighting? were they not idle and dull?" asked Theodore.

"Certainly not. None of the soldiers of Gustavus Adolphus were allowed to remain idle. When not engaged in active service, the men became pioneers and military architects. Each soldier was his own tailor and mechanic, or mended his clothes, when necessary; it was not at all an unusual sight to see them knitting or making lace."

"O grandpapa! but of course the officers did not do such things as that?"

"Yes, Eric, I know they did," exclaimed Ulrica; "for those beautiful point-lace ruffles which grandpapa wears sometimes, he told me he made himself after some great battle."

Eric looked perplexed. "Why, grandpapa," he said, "I have always heard that the Swedish soldiers of Gustavus Adolphus were among the bravest in the world. How could they do such work?"

"Because it was better than doing nothing, my boy. I have often looked with pleasure on those hardy soldiers, the victors in a hundred fights, as they sat quietly knitting their own stockings, or making lace to be sent as a remembrance to their Swedish homes. Such employment did not make them the less brave. Their valor, hardihood, and humanity, were extolled throughout Europe. Alike patient of summer heat and winter cold, frugal, temperate, and highly disciplined, our Swedish soldiers might well be deemed examples of what soldiers should be. It was King Gustavus who had brought the army into this state—King Gustavus, whom we almost idolized—and who marched through Germany as a conqueror, the sword in one hand, and mercy in the other. All that could be done to lessen the calamities attendant on war, he did—the most humane, the most merciful, the most pious of conquerors, was truly Gustavus Adolphus the Great!"

"Did not the Austrians call him the Snow King?" asked Eva.

"Yes; they thought he would, with his army, speedily melt away before the fiery forces of the south; but they were mistaken. The Snow King, with his dauntless spirit and military skill, took town after town, and city after city—freed the oppressed Protestants in Germany from the Austrian yoke, and astonished all Europe by the success of his arms. The battles of Leipsic, of the Leech, and of Lutzen, proved the Snow King of the North to be very powerful."

"Ah! I know at the first two he defeated the Austrian general, Count Tilly, and at Lutzen he fought with General Wallenstein. I want you to tell me something about that extraordinary man, if you please."

"Yes, Fred, but grandpapa was going to tell us of the two boys first."

"True, so I was, Eric. I had often noticed the two brothers for their serious and proper attention at divine service, and for their affectionate behavior to each other. They were orphans; their father fell in battle, and King Gustavus, taking the children under his special protection, had them trained up beneath his own eye. Early accustomed to the employments of a military life, taught patiently to endure cold, hunger, and fatigue, brought up in habits of strict obedience, while at the same time the importance of truth, and the duties of kindness and humanity were impressed upon them, Charles and Gustaf gave ample promise of becoming brave and good soldiers. They were favorites with the whole army, though so young; King Gustavus himself often kindly noticed the orphans of Leipsic, as they were called. Well, as I told you, public schools were opened every day with the same regularity and quiet as in one of our country towns, and the moment the forces began to intrench themselves, the children went to a safe and peaceable quarter, marked out as their place of study. It happened one day, that I was visiting the school at the time when some little rewards of merit were being distributed among the boys.

I observed that though one was presented to Gustaf, he did not seem particularly pleased, but when a similar one was given to his brother, his countenance brightened up wonderfully.

"'Ah that is right!' he exclaimed, 'now I am so glad! Are we not happy, Charlie?'

"'What makes you so happy, my boy?' I asked. 'Have you never had a reward of merit before?'

"'O yes, sir; the reason I am glad, is because in a few days the king will visit us, and he always inquires to whom the rewards have been given, and I should have been so very, very sorry if Charlie and I had not each one to show him.'

"'Why should you have been sorry?' I said.

"'Ah sir!' exclaimed both the boys, 'King Gustavus would have thought we had not tried to please him, and we do indeed love him from our hearts. He has been so good and kind to us!'

"'He is a good king, truly,' I observed; 'I trust you will make him two brave soldiers.'

"'I hope so,' replied Gustaf; 'I would do anything for him. How happy I should be to die in saving his life! Charlie, shall you ever forget the day when we first saw him? how the tears stood in his eyes as he said, "Be good boys, my children, and I will be a father to you." He has indeed been a father to us both!'

"'Yes, and he told us always to trust in God, and pray devoutly to him, for we could neither be good nor happy unless we did. I have never forgotten that. But see, Gustaf, the classes are forming.'

"It was pleasing to a soldier's eye to observe the quick and orderly formation of the various classes. Each boy fell into his place in an instant, without a word being spoken; and the steady attention which the little fellows gave to their lessons was quite remarkable. Gustaf and Charles, in particular, appeared to have no thoughts but for the task assigned them. Their bright and happy countenances, as side by side they looked over the same book, bespoke much intellect and sweetness of disposition; and I turned to the master to make some inquiries as to their progress in learning. His account was most satisfactory. 'They are the best boys in my school,' he said; 'in obedience, diligence, and kindness of heart, none can equal them, and the motive which animates them to do well, is that of pleasing our good king. He has quite won their hearts by his kindness to them, and I will venture to say, that when these boys grow up, King Gustavus will not have, in his whole army, braver soldiers or better men than they will be.' I was about to reply, when a sudden and loud crash was heard—I well knew the sound. In anxious alarm I looked around—alas! the orphan brothers and two of their companions lay dead upon the floor!"

"O, grandpapa! what was it? what killed them?"

"A cannon-ball had pierced the school-house, and done its dreadful errand. The general, who had allotted out the ground, thought it secure from the enemy's guns, for every precaution was taken to insure the safety of the children. But he was mistaken, and four out of that youthful group were in a moment hurried into eternity!"

"How very dreadful!" exclaimed little Eva. "I suppose all the other boys ran away directly?"

"On the contrary, not one stirred from his place. In such good discipline were these young soldiers, that not a pen or a book dropped from their hands, not a word was spoken, nor did one even change color But I noticed many eyes filled with tears as they gazed on the lifeless bodies of their favorite companions, so lately in health and spirits by their side."

"Was King Gustavus very sorry when he heard of their sad fate?"

"He was deeply grieved. 'Alas! my orphan children!' he exclaimed; 'I have in them lost two brave and faithful soldiers!' By his orders, a solemn hymn was chanted over their graves, as they were committed to the earth amidst the tears of the regiment."

"Poor little boys!" said Ulrica; "what a terrible destruction a cannon-ball makes!"

"A very short time after this, I was riding with the king, who was reconnoitering the enemy, when a ball passed through the body of the horse on which he was mounted. Immediately falling with its rider, it was several times rolled over and over upon the earth by the violence of the shock. After extricating the king from his dead steed, I found he had happily received no injury, except that the skin of his foot had been slightly rased by the shot. He was calm and unmoved, but said, 'I have had a fortunate escape, and a fresh warning to be prepared for that fate which may meet me at any moment, and to which I am as liable as the meanest of my soldiers. I resign myself to the will of Divine Providence.' A few minutes after, a cannon shot carried off the head of a young officer, much beloved by the king and the whole army. His father, an aged nobleman, who had distinguished himself in the Thirty Years' War, on receiving the intelligence, said to the friends who were endeavoring to console him, 'I am a father, my friends, it is true;

but I am at the same time a Christian. My son belonged to God before he belonged to me.'"

"O, I do not like to hear of people killing each other so," said Eva. "Can you not tell us something else, dear grandpapa?"

"Shall I tell you about Queen Eleanora, who loved her husband so tenderly? She liked fighting as little as you do, Eva, but as Gustavus was absent so long in Germany, she determined to follow him thither. Accordingly, she left the pleasures of Stockholm, and went to Germany, taking with her no inconsiderable supply of men, artillery, and money. During her short stay at Stettin, she expressed a wish that all the grand fêtes and entertainments prepared in honor of her arrival might be dispensed with. 'I do not think it right,' she said, 'that I should spend my time in diversions, while my dear husband is exposing his life to perils in the field; I should much prefer, if it please you, seeing the money intended to be laid out for my amusement expended in the offices of charity.' She traversed Germany to meet the king, and at Leipsic was received with extraordinary honors; that Protestant city presenting her, as the wife of the deliverer of Germany, with a copy of the Bible, and a service of silver. Wherever she went, she was gratified by hearing from every mouth the praises of a husband whom she loved with an intense affection. The meeting of the royal pair was a most interesting and touching scene. Though it took place in public, and the king was surrounded by princes and officers, Eleanora, with a transport of joy I cannot describe, flew to him, threw her arms round his neck, and exclaimed with tears of delight, 'The great Gustavus is indeed taken prisoner at last!'"

"Was it not Queen Eleanora who gave you the Order of the Golden Heart, grandpapa?"

"It was. When our beloved king fell at Lutzen, the sad intelligence threw the poor queen almost into a state of distraction. For a long time her grief was inconsolable, and for months after the funeral solemnities were performed, she continued to keep in her chamber a golden box containing the heart of her deceased husband. This she visited with tears and lamentations many times in the day, till the senate, fearing such indulgence of sorrow might injure her health, induced her to consent to its interment, when she instituted, in memory of the circumstance, the celebrated Order of the Golden Heart."

"And that is the medal we have seen you wear? Well, I do not wonder Queen Eleanora loved Gustavus; but he would have wished her to be more resigned to the divine will, would he not?"

"He himself showed much resignation and trust in God, in all the events of life. I remember once being in some anxiety as to the future, and I suppose, was looking troubled, when King Gustavus came up to me, and with a kindly smile, laying his hand on my shoulder, said in the words of his grandfather, Gustavus Vasa,—

'Thou Swede, put firmly thy trust in God,
And ardently wait thou upon him.'

My heart felt lighter in a moment."

"What a different man King Gustavus was from the cruel Wallenstein!"

"Different indeed! Wallenstein was remarkable for his haughty temper, and aspiring disposition. He was possessed of such immense wealth, that his palace could vie in costly splendor with that of any monarch in Europe. His table, in splendid array, was generally furnished with covers for a hundred guests. An armed guard of fifty men was stationed in his ante-chamber, while six barons, six knights, and no less than sixty pages, were in dayly attendance on him. The most gorgeous dresses were worn by his servants, and his chamberlains were equipped with chains and keys of massive gold. I have been told that the stalls in his stable were of Bohemian marble, and the racks and mangers of polished steel. When he traveled, his attendants and baggage occupied a hundred wagons, and the gentlemen of his court sixty coaches. His manner was stern and repulsive. When *he* gave orders, woe to him who should dare to disobey! It is said, that one of his pages happening to awake him somewhat earlier than the appointed time, he had him immediately executed. On the other hand, he generally rewarded prompt obedience. Having issued an order that no scarfs but those of a scarlet color were to be worn by his officers, a captain, who was present, to show his obedience to the mandate, immediately tore from his neck one which was handsomely embroidered in various colors, and trampled it under his feet. Wallenstein at once raised him to the rank of colonel."

"His officers could not love him, grandpapa?"

"No; he was well obeyed, from fear, but he was without a single friend. Though he paid his soldiers liberally, and made magnificent presents, no one loved him. Pillage, as you know, was strictly forbidden by our beloved king. Wallenstein, on the contrary, offered the emperor to raise an army of fifty thousand men at his own expense, provided they should support themselves by plunder in the hostile countries!"

"Had he not, at times, a great aversion to noise?"

"So great, that the streets near his castle were barricaded with strong bars and chains, and sentinels placed on purpose to preserve perfect silence; while the officers who were admitted to his presence were obliged to prevent the jingling of their spurs, by tying silk twist around them."

"What a selfish, cruel man he was," observed Ulrica. "I suppose he was very angry when he was defeated at Lutzen?"

"Yes; he cruelly had several of his brave officers executed on the public scaffold, on a charge of cowardice in that battle. His conduct was uniformly so strange, that King Gustavus in general spoke of him as 'the madman.'"

"And he called Count Tilly, 'the old corporal.' I remember he was slain at the famous battle of the Lech. He must have been a brave old general."

"O! Frederick," said Olga, "I never hear his name without thinking of the terrible siege of Magdeburg. How *very* cruel and barbarous Tilly's soldiers were when he took that city!"

"Pray do not talk of the siege of Magdeburg," said little Eva, "it makes me shudder to think of it. Nurse was living there at the time, and she told me one day about its horrors, but I never wish to hear any more. Could you not tell us another little story about good King Gustavus, dear grandpapa?"

The old general smiled. "Well, dear Eva," he said, after a pause, "I will tell you about his being very angry with grandpapa."

"Could that be?" said the little girl, opening her eyes in surprise; "I always thought he was very kind to you."

"And I have always heard that General Arnheim was one of his favorite officers," observed Frederic.

"That may be, dear children; but if General Arnheim did wrong, was King Gustavus to pass it by? No; beloved as he was by every Swedish heart, he would not have possessed the affections of his people as he did, had he made laws which he suffered to be broken with impunity."

"Did *you* break his laws, grandpapa?'

"You shall hear. Dueling was a custom prevalent throughout Europe at that time. For the least affront, intentional or not, men took offense, a challenge was given, and a duel fought. So universal was this mode of settling quarrels, that in France alone, during the reign of Henry the Fourth, no less than four thousand of the nobility were slain in duels. The custom was spreading fast among us, and he, who for the very slightest affront, was not willing to give or to accept a challenge, was deemed a coward. Gustavus Adolphus, determined to put a stop to a practice which he considered both absurd and murderous, made a law that he who fought a duel, on any pretense whatever, should be punished with death. At the same time, he established a court of honor, composed of the principal officers of the army, to decide upon those questions which hitherto had been settled by the sword, and after a fair trial, an apology was ordered to be made on the part of him who had given offense. Some few months after this law was made, it happened that I fell into a dispute with a brother officer about some trifle; words ran high, and in the heat of temper he gave, and I accepted, a challenge. The words had scarcely passed my lips, when I felt I had done wrong; but I had allowed my passion to get the better of me, and I was too proud then to acknowledge it. Well aware that the duel could not be fought without the king's knowledge, and certain that such an offense would not be passed by, we somewhat boldly resolved to go to our sovereign and ask his permission to settle our dispute with the sword. The king heard us with calm surprise, but, concealing his indignation, replied, 'Your request, I confess, has rather astonished me, gentlemen. It is an unexpected one; but you seem much in earnest on the subject, and doubtless are convinced, that by one killing the other, the point in dispute will be effectually settled. I am unwilling to refuse what two of my most experienced generals and faithful officers ask of me. You know my opinions on dueling,—but your request is granted; and I myself will be a witness to your spirit and valor on the occasion. It would be a pity for your king to miss seeing a fight between two of his bravest subjects.' We retired, not very certain whether the king approved of our conduct or not. Though dignified and polite, his manner wanted that kindness and affability which usually marked it when he spoke to any of his old officers. However, it was too late to retract, though a pang shot through my heart, at the thought that I might have displeased my gracious sovereign. To be sure that I had not fallen in my master's favor, to have seen him look kindly on me, as usual, I felt that I could have made any reasonable apology to a brother officer, or submitted to the court of judges any insult that I might have received."

"But why did you not make an apology, then, dear grandpapa?" inquired Theodore, eagerly.

"My dear boy, I was too proud to do so.

I felt I had done wrong, but I could not acknowledge it, and, like every one else who feels that, I was not happy. However, my pride brought its own punishment with it. At the appointed hour, on the day named, General Bergstrom and myself, well armed and attended, presented ourselves at the place of meeting. Scarcely had we arrived, when King Gustavus galloped up, at the head of a body of infantry, which he immediately formed in a circle round the spot. There was a look of stern determination, and, I thought, displeasure, on his brow. After the necessary preparations had been made, as we stood confronting each other, with our weapons drawn, ready to commence the combat, our attention was arrested by the appearance of a man, who, with a heavy saber in his hand, walked into the ring, and stood as if to watch the proceedings. The king observed our astonishment, and riding forwards, said, in a tone of marked displeasure, 'Do not be surprised, gentlemen. According to the laws of your country, your lives are already forfeited in consequence of the offense to which you have endeavored to make me a party. You will therefore take notice, that the instant one falls by the sword of his antagonist, the executioner, who stands there, has my orders to strike off the head of the other. My laws are not to be trifled with thus.' The words seemed to bring us to our senses. Struck with shame at our conduct, we knelt at the feet of our sovereign and entreated his forgiveness. 'It is granted,' said Gustavus Adolphus, 'on one condition—that you instantly become reconciled to each other, and that you give me your solemn word to refrain from such acts of disobedience for the future.' Receiving forgiveness from the king, we readily forgave each other, feeling ashamed that a trifling quarrel should have disturbed a friendship of many years.

"On our giving the required promise, Gustavus's brow cleared. 'I can trust you,' he said; 'but I declare, before you all, I will not again pass over an offense of this kind. The law shall take effect, and death shall be the punishment of the duelist. It is my wish to have soldiers under my command, not gladiators. If any one wishes to prove to his fellow-countrymen that he is no coward, let him do so on the field of battle.'

"Such, my dear children, was the circumstance. It was the only time in which I ever remember to have fallen under the king's displeasure, and I was taught a lesson then that I never forgot in after life."

"Had King Gustavus any children?" said Eva.

"He had one little daughter, named Christina, of whom he was very fond. I first saw her at Calmar. She was then only two years of age, and the governor hesitated to give the king the usual salute, lest the noise of the cannon might terrify the child. Gustavus being informed of it, exclaimed, 'Fire! the girl is the daughter of a soldier, and must be accustomed early to such sounds.' Instead of being frightened, however, little Christina clapped her hands, and cried, 'More! more!'"

"And when did you see her again, grandpapa?"

"I saw her again when King Gustavus took leave of the Estates before going to Germany. Taking the child in his arms, he presented her to the assembled deputies as their future sovereign. He spoke of the probability of his falling in battle, and commended his infant daughter to the protection of his faithful subjects in such terms as to draw tears from the eyes of all present. One after another, the deputies advanced, and kneeling before the little Christina, took the oath of allegiance to her as their future queen. After a parting address to the several orders of the state present,—a farewell which will never be forgotten by those who heard it,—the king presided at a splendid banquet, delighting all by the kindness and affability of his manner, no less than by the intelligence of his conversation. He then prepared for embarkation, and while giving us the requisite orders, the Princess Christina approached for the purpose of delivering a little speech upon his departure, in which she had been carefully instructed. The king, busy with the scene before him, was not aware of the child's presence, till she had two or three times pulled him by the coat, to attract his attention. Turning suddenly round, Gustavus beheld his infant daughter in the attitude of commencing her address. With a burst of uncontrollable emotion he caught her up in his arms, bestowed on her many caresses, and hung over her for a long time in tears, as if willing to defer to the last moment the pang of separation. It was an affecting scene. The brave warrior and tender father parted with his only—his loved child—never to see her more!"

"O, I am glad my papa does not go to war, and leave me," said Eva. "But can you tell us anything more about Christina?"

"She was only six years old when, by the lamented death of her father, she became Queen of Sweden. Of course, she had guardians, of whom the wise and prudent Chancellor Oxenstiern was at the head. Her education was rather a masculine one. She was instructed in Latin, Greek, Hebrew, history, and politics, while her amusements were riding, hunting, shooting, and reviewing troops. At the age of eighteen she took the reins of government."

"And she resigned them the very day I was four years old, because she was tired of being a queen. That is six years ago," said Frederic.

"How old was Christina then, Theodore, when she grew weary of royalty?"

"She was only eight-and-twenty. And she gave the crown to her cousin, our present king, Charles the Tenth."

"Queen Christina was not a good queen, was she, grandpapa?"

"I grieve to say she was not, Ulrica. But reverence and affection for her father's memory stifled all murmurs from her subjects. One action of hers would have deeply pained our Protestant king. After her abdication, she forsook the religion which he had so nobly upheld, and became a Roman Catholic. Her great desire was to make a sensation in the world, and she has succeeded; but her extraordinary conduct has only gained her pity, contempt, and dislike. Vain, ridiculous, and unhappy, she is living at Rome, an unworthy daughter of the great Gustavus Adolphus."

"I think it was rather amusing that the Austrians should give our brave monarch the title of 'The Snow King,' when his armies did not melt away, as they expected. The name of the 'Lion of the North' might well be his."

General Arnheim smiled on his animated little grandson. "Now, my dear children," said he, "before we say goodnight, I should like to hear a chant. What shall it be?"

"Shall we sing King Gustavus's own hymn,—

'Be not afraid, thou little band?'"

said Olga.

"A chant, if you please," cried several voices. "The same that our Swedish soldiers chanted before the battle of Lutzen."

"Very well; now then, do your best."

And in sweet, clear tones, the children all joined in chanting Martin Luther's celebrated paraphrase of the forty-sixth Psalm, commencing with—

"God is our strong tower of refuge."

And so their pleasant day concluded.

Early on the following morning, Frederic repaired to the nursery. "Good-morning, nurse Christy," he said to a cheerful-looking woman; "we are going to have such a treat to-day!"

"Indeed, sir! and what may that be?"

"Why, we are all going, in so many sledges, across the lake. I am so delighted!"

"Across the lake, Maeler! that will be a nice excursion truly! but I must wrap up my little girls well, then."

"Well, nurse, you could not wrap them up much more than you do, I think. Fur pelisses, fur bonnets, fur shoes, fur gloves, and fur muffs, besides tippets, and vails, and handkerchiefs; what more can they wear?"

"Ah! twenty miles is a long way for little Eva to go," said nurse, shaking her head; "I must take care of her."

"It is well we are not going up the lake, that would be eighty miles, you know. Nurse Christy, Eva said you remembered something about the siege of Magdeburg."

"I shall never forget it if I lived a hundred years, Master Frederic," said nurse with a sigh.

"Is it not at Magdeburg there is such a fine cathedral?" said Frederic.

"Yes, sir; they say it was one hundred and fifty years in building. It is very magnificent, and has two steeples three hundred and fifty feet in height."

"What was there so very dreadful in the siege, nurse? I always thought it a very fine exploit to besiege and take a town."

"O, sir, you would never think so again if you once could see what I have seen! The fair city of Magdeburg, after being taken by Count Tilly, was given over to pillage, then set on fire, and thirty thousand of the inhabitants put to the sword. The whole town, except the cathedral, one church, and a few houses, was reduced to ashes. Alas! for the well-fortified and fair city of Magdeburg!"

"What made Tilly besiege it?"

"It was a Protestant city, and had declared for Gustavus Adolphus. The King of Sweden, however, was too far off to save us, and after a long siege Magdeburg fell into the hands of the Austrians."

"Were you in the town at the time, nurse Christy?"

"Yes, master Fred, I was a little girl at school. One morning, just as we had assembled, some one, running in, told us the city was taken:—'Shut your books, and run home, my children,' said our master, 'and pray to God to protect you.'"

"We ran into the street, all dispersing different ways. I had long been terrified by the thundering of the cannon against the city walls, but I saw now there was something more fearful than that. I had only gone a few steps when I met a little child about two years old, walking alone. As it stopped to play with something, a soldier, running by, killed it with his sword. Struck with horror at the sight, I concealed myself in a doorway. O, to what cruel scenes I was a witness! The

Austrian soldiers murdered all who came in their way, man, woman, and child. I would have given all I possessed to have been safe at home. Trembling and crying, I at last ventured on. I had not gone far before I saw a party of soldiers approaching, and opening the first shop-door I came to, I ran in. An old man was there, who, with trembling fingers, was putting some money and jewels in a box. He did not see me, and not able to speak from fright, I hid myself behind a large cask. Just as I had done so, the soldiers rushed in. 'Deliver up your money!' they exclaimed to the old man, 'or you have not a moment to live.' The poor man gave up all his wealth."

"'Is this all you have?' said the ruffians.

"'All I have in the world,' he replied.

"They laughed, took the treasure, and shot him dead!"

"O, how dreadful! how cruel!" exclaimed Frederic.

"Ah! I saw worse deeds of cruelty than that, sir; but I will not shock you by an account of them. The houses were all entered and ransacked, and the children murdered, as they clung to their mothers for protection. Twenty young ladies, overcome with fright, jumped into the Elbe. The bloodshed, the terror, the screams, the confusion, and the fire, formed a scene which was indeed terrible to contemplate, and fearful to look back upon."

"Did you reach home in safety, nurse?"

"I did, sir, after many escapes. Once a soldier, holding me up by the hair of my head, was about to kill me, when he caught sight of a man trying to escape with some treasure, and he left me to seize it. I reached home, but it was deserted, and I have never since that terrible day heard any tidings of my father, mother, or sister."

"Have you not, nurse Christy? O, that is very sad! What should I have done if my dear father or darling sister had perished in the siege of Magdeburg! I did not know sieges were such horrible things."

"Alas! that is because they sound fine to talk about. Sieges and battles are, in my opinion, very unfit for men professing

Christianity. Sometimes, I suppose, they can scarcely be avoided; but I doubt not, as the world grows older, men will grow wiser, and not live to kill each other. King Gustavus, soldier as he was, shed tears at the fate of Magdeburg."

By this time the gay sledges were at the door, and Frederic, giving nurse Christy a bright ribbon for her cap, ran off to join the happy party.

He thought, as he drove along, of what he had heard, and was a little shaken in his determination to be a soldier.

I hope all little children who read this story, join heart and lip in the prayer so often offered up in Christian churches,— "*That it may please the Lord to give all nations unity, peace, and concord.*"

The Iron Ring.

One cold winter's morning, a little boy, about seven years of age, was taking a ride in the vicinity of Stockholm. The capital of Sweden is in a situation remarkable for its romantic scenery. It is built on seven small rocky islands, which are connected by bridges; and numerous rocks of granite, rising boldly from the surface of the water, partly bare and craggy, and partly dotted with houses or feathered with wood, have a very picturesque effect. The harbor is an inlet of the Baltic, and the water is so deep that ships of the largest size can approach the quay. At its extremity rises the city, street above street, in the form of an amphitheater; and the palace, a magnificent building, crowns the summit. All was now ice and snow, and every one was warmly wrapped up in furs. The little boy, as he looked around him, saw no gal-

CHARLES THE TWELFTH.

See page 117.

lant ships sailing into the harbor, for the Baltic Sea was frozen over, and now there was skating on it, races in sledges and various games. Here came a sledge rapidly along, with two men in it well muffled up: and by the gratulations they received on all sides, it was evident they had crossed the Baltic. Some of the sledges were very elegant, with their gayly caparisoned horses and tinkling sleigh bells; and gracefully they skimmed along over the ice.

Should you like to live in one of those cold countries, with its long, long winter? The Swedish children have not the amusements you have, but they are very happy and contented. When the father of a little family has been out all day in the ice and snow, how the children watch for his return as the evening draws in! and how quick are their ears to catch the first sound of the distant sleigh bells! Then may the grateful mother sing—

" 'T is merry to hear at evening time,
By the blazing hearth, the sleigh bells chime;
To know each bound of the steed brings near
The form of him to our bosoms dear:

Lightly we spring the fire to raise,
Till the rafters glow with the ruddy blaze.

"'T is he! and blithely the gay bells sound,
As his steed skims over the frozen ground;
Hark! he has pass'd the gloomy wood,
He crosses now the ice-bound flood,
And sees the light from the open door,
To hail his toilsome journey o'er.

"Our hut is small, and rude our cheer,
But love has spread the banquet here;
And childhood springs to be caress'd
By our beloved and welcome guest;
With smiling brow his tale he tells,
They, laughing, ring the merry bells.

"From the gloomy wood the wolf may howl;
From the blasted pine loud whoop the owl;
The sudden crash of the falling tree
Is sound of terror no more to me;
No longer I list with boding fear
The sleigh bells' merry peal to hear."

But we must return to the little Swede. The pony on which he was mounted was a spirited animal, and had more than once that morning attempted to run away; but the child, who perfectly understood the art of managing him, held him in with a tight rein. Indeed, it was astonishing to see one so young ride so well, and have such a command over his pony. Now he would put him to a quick gallop, then cause him to trot gently, and at last he made him leap over a wall. This feat, however, the pony seemed determined not to accomplish, but his little master was quite as determined that he should. Again and again did he spur him on to the attempt, and again and again did the pony start aside from making it. "You will not conquer *me*," said the boy quietly; and at length, after a contest which lasted nearly an hour, the leap was made, greatly to the delight of the attendant groom, who, however, was too respectful to express his admiration. And Charles, (for that was the name of the resolute young rider,) having repeated the leap two or three times, exulting in the mastery he had obtained over his pony, rode home at a gallop.

Little Charles did not like reading, or learning lessons, but he was very fond of riding, skating, firing off cannon, or anything relating to a military life. He was brought up in a very hardy manner, and accustomed from an early age to suffer patiently cold, hunger, fatigue, and pain. He was not daunted by difficulties; and as to fear, he did not know its name.

But Charles was very obstinate. At times, nothing could bend his stubborn will. Punishments he did not fear; entreaties he did not regard;—there was but one thing which had any effect on him when in these obstinate moods; and that was, *the love of glory.* This motive governed him all his life, and a very bad, unworthy motive it was.

One day, after his tutor had been in vain endeavoring to persuade him to apply to Latin, which nothing could induce him to learn, Charles exclaimed, "What *can* be the use of learning such a dry, dead language? What glory will it be to understand Latin?"

"You would not wish to be more ignorant than others," replied the tutor; "the king of Denmark and the king of Poland both understand Latin; would you be behind them?"

"Behind them!" exclaimed Charles,

"no, in no one thing will I be behind them! Give me the book, I will at once begin." And in a very short time he learned the language so well as to be able to converse in it.

Another day, as he was reading the Life of Alexander the Great, his tutor asked what he thought of him. "I think," said Charles, "I should like to resemble him."

"But he died at the early age of thirty-three."

"Ah!" said Charles, "and was not his life long enough, when he had conquered kingdoms?"

When he was eleven years old, this same boy lost his mother, and four years afterward, his father also; and, now aged fifteen, was crowned king of Sweden, under the title of Charles the Twelfth. He was one of the most extraordinary kings that ever reigned.

His grandmother, the widow of Charles the Tenth, had been left regent of the kingdom, and not a little pleased was she with her new dignity, which she hoped might long continue.

Charles the Eleventh had in his will desired that his son should not assume the reins of government till the age of eighteen; and the young king passed his time in hunting, reviewing his troops, and the various military exercises in which he delighted. As he appeared quite happy with these amusements, the old queen looked forward to long enjoying the sweets of authority. She was, however, disappointed.

One day, a few months after the death of his father, Charles was returning from the review of several of his regiments, with the counselor of state, Piper, by his side. He rode slowly, and appeared to be thinking deeply. After some time Piper said, "May I take the liberty of asking the subject of your majesty's meditation?"

"I am thinking," replied the king, "that I am worthy of governing these brave troops myself; and I wish neither myself nor them any longer to receive orders from a woman."

Piper acted upon these words, and in three days Charles the Twelfth, at the early age of fifteen, took the government of his kingdom; while the old queen, mortified and disappointed at such a sudden end being put to her power, retired to a private life.

On the day of his coronation, the young king entered Stockholm on a bay horse ornamented with silver trappings; and, the scepter in his hand, and the crown upon his head, he rode along the streets of his capital, amid the acclamations of assembled thousands, and loud shouts of "Long live King Charles the Twelfth!"

"He is young," said an old man, "but not too young to reign. There is something about him which leads me to hope he will almost equal the great Gustavus."

"Nay," said another, "he may be as brave, but I doubt if he has his kind and gentle disposition."

"Or his piety and trust in God," observed a third.

At the ceremony of the coronation, as the Archbishop of Upsal, in right of his office, was proceeding to place the crown on the king's head, Charles took it out of his hands and crowned himself, at the same time giving the archbishop a stern and haughty look.

"He will be a king in earnest," whispered one of the attendants to another. "Take my word for it, no one will govern Charles the Twelfth."

In a small town of Saxony, two officers once met for the first time. The meeting was apparently a friendly, and evidently an expected one. One of the officers was of a noble and commanding figure, but with a stern expression of countenance; though his clear blue eyes gave a softness, and his fine forehead a dignity to his features. He was dressed in a coat of coarse blue cloth, with large gilt buttons, thick buff-leather gloves, which reached nearly to the elbow, and a pair of immense boots; while in his hand he carried a very long sword. The other officer wore his regimentals; his countenance was pleasing, and his manners polished and gentle.

The first was King Charles the Twelfth

of Sweden, the latter, Augustus, King of Poland.

Now though these two monarchs had fought against each other in battle — though Charles had taken the crown of Poland from Augustus — though they had heard of each other, and thought of each other for a long period, — yet, now when they met for the first time, the conversation turned chiefly on the great boots of the Swedish king! "Indeed," said Augustus, smiling, "I cannot but admire your majesty's boots; I have often heard of them, but they exceed my expectations."

"Are they not capital?" replied Charles; "I have not taken them off for six years, but when I went to bed."

The monarchs afterward dined together, and no one would have imagined from the calm self-possession of Augustus, that he was in company with one who had not only done him a great injury, and heaped on him cruel mortifications, but was meditating yet more.

"I am glad I have seen the famous King of Sweden," said little Albert Leipholt, as he walked with his father along the banks of the winding river, on the evening of this day; "but I think I should be rather afraid of him. What a great sword he had in his hand!"

"That was the sword he used at Narva, my boy, when with eight thousand Swedes he defeated eighty thousand Russians."

"What a brave conqueror! But, papa, why does he not stay in Sweden and govern it?"

"Because he is fond of glory, and to obtain it he goes to war with other nations."

"But does that do any good?"

"No, it does a great deal of harm, both to Sweden and the countries where the war is carried on. Some of King Charles's ministers lately advised him to return to his own kingdom, which was in a sad state without its sovereign; but he is very obstinate, and replied, 'If I were to remain here fifty years, I will not go till I have dethroned the King of Poland.'"

"And has he deposed him?"

"He has. But when Count Piper

advised him to place the crown on his own head, he replied, 'It is more glory to give away than to gain a kingdom,' and caused Stanislaus, a Polish palatine, to be elected king."

"He had no right to give away what did not belong to him, however," said Albert. "Papa, I do not like Charles the Twelfth at all."

"Yet he has many good qualities, Albert, one of which is, that he has never been known to break his word. His army also is well disciplined; he does not allow his soldiers to pillage the towns they take. At our great fair of Leipsic the other day, not a single Swedish soldier was to be seen in it, though Charles's army was encamped in the neighborhood. The merchants went in perfect safety to the fair, Charles saying that he and his troops were only here to watch over the peace of the country."

"But our beautiful country belongs to King Augustus; we do not want the Swedes to protect us."

"The Swedish king thought differently.

One day, as he was riding near Leipsic, one of our Saxon peasants threw himself on his knees before him, demanding justice on a soldier who had taken away the dinner provided for his family. Charles desired the soldier to come before him, and with a severe countenance asked him if he had dared to rob the man. 'Sire,' replied the soldier, 'I have not done him so much injury as you have done his master; you took away a kingdom from him, I have taken but a turkey from this peasant.'"

"That was a clever answer for the soldier to make."

"I suppose Charles thought so too, for when he had given ten ducats to the peasant, he pardoned the soldier, saying at the same time, 'Remember, friend, though I took a kingdom from Augustus, I kept nothing for myself.'"

"Did Augustus fight for his kingdom, papa?"

"Very bravely. He did all that a king could do, but success attended the arms of the conquering Swede. Nothing seems to stop his progress, while the rapidity with which he moves his troops is astonishing. If a river comes in their way, they swim across it; and Charles at the head of his cavalry once marched ninety miles in twenty-four hours, each soldier having a horse by his side, on which to mount when his own was tired. Augustus fought in vain; unable to contend with so powerful an adversary, he was reluctantly compelled to sue for peace. This was granted, but only on the most humiliating terms."

"What were they, dear papa?"

"The first condition was, that Augustus should renounce forever the crown of Poland, that he should acknowledge Stanislaus as the lawful king, and that he should promise never to think of reascending the throne, even after the death of Stanislaus. When the Polish nobles endeavored to obtain terms a little less severe for their king, Count Piper answered very quietly, 'Such is the will of my master, and he never changes his resolution.'"

"What an arbitrary, self-willed man he must be!"

"He obliged Augustus also to send to Stanislaus all the crown jewels; and I heard to-day he intends to make him write a letter to the new king, and congratulate him on his elevation to the throne of Poland."

"Well, if I were Augustus, I *would not* do that, however."

"If Charles orders, he will be obeyed. He is the conqueror, and Augustus the conquered. The deposed monarch is also himself to give order that his name, as King of Poland, shall in future be omitted in the public prayers."

"Papa, I only wonder that King Augustus could dine with King Charles to-day, and be so calm and polite to him."

"He has too much amiability and self-possession to lose the command of his temper, or to be otherwise than polite. Charles was polite also; it would have been very unkingly to be rude."

"See, papa! here they come."

Little Albert and his father had wandered into some private pleasure grounds, at the back of the house where the monarchs had dined together, when, rather to their surprise, on turning down a walk, they saw them approaching with one or two attendants. They were conversing pleasantly with each other, and admiring the golden sunset. The Saxon officer and his little son stood respectfully on one side to let them pass. The King of Sweden returned his salute, and looked kindly on the child; while King Augustus said in his usual affable manner, "Ah! Leipholt, is that you? it is long since we met. And this is your little boy? Be a good son," he continued, as he kindly patted Albert's fair head, "be a good son, and God will bless you."

The monarchs passed on; but Albert gazed at King Charles's jack-boots till they were out of sight.

"Papa!" said the little boy as they walked home, "it is a pity the King of Sweden is so fond of glory. His subjects may think him a very wonderful man and a great conqueror, but they cannot love him as we love King Augustus, or as the Swedes loved the great Gustavus Adolphus."

"And yet he thinks he imitates his celebrated ancestor. A short time since he visited the plains of Lutzen, where the Swedish hero fell. On the fatal spot being pointed out to him, he gazed at it with interest, exclaiming, 'I have endeavored to live his life; may God grant me one day as glorious a death!' But Charles the Twelfth lives to advance his own glory; Gustavus Adolphus had a higher motive to actuate him."

In the south of Russia, before the strong town of Pultowa, which belonged to the Czar, was a besieging army. This town was well stored with provisions and other necessaries, and it was also well defended by a garrison of nine hundred men. Though in a wild and rugged country—though with half-famished troops—though surrounded with dangers and difficulties—the leader of that besieging host, undaunted and undismayed, hoped not only to take Pultowa, but to defeat and dethrone the Czar. He was riding one morning to give orders for a fresh assault, when he was told the Czar approached with seventy thousand men. "Very well," he replied, "it will save us the trouble of going to him. He comes to be defeated." He continued his ride, and after a sharp skirmish with the enemy, was returning to the camp, when a musket ball pierced his boot, and shattered the bone of his heel. Not the slightest change, however, was visible on his countenance, and no one could have suspected for a moment that he was wounded. He gave his orders with the greatest composure, and remained on horseback for six hours longer. One of his attendants at length perceiving that his boot was covered with blood, ran to fetch the surgeons. "Haste! haste!" he cried, "the king is wounded!" In the mean time the pain had become so great, that the royal sufferer was obliged to be assisted in a fainting state from his horse, and carried into his tent. Can you guess who it was that endured pain so well? Charles the Twelfth of Sweden.

As soon as he was laid upon a couch the surgeons examined the wound. They looked concerned, and consulted together in whispers.

"Well," said Charles, "what is the matter?"

The surgeons hesitated a reply.

"Come, tell me at once; what is it? Must the leg be taken off?"

"Indeed, your majesty, we fear so," they answered; "there appears to be no other course left; the wound is a very severe one."

The king was silent; but while all in the tent appeared alarmed and agitated, he alone was calm and unmoved.

The news soon spread through the army that Charles was wounded, and about to have his leg amputated. Great was the consternation of the soldiers at the sad tidings.

"How shall we meet the Czar," they said, "without our king to head us in battle? How can we conquer without the presence of our victorious leader?"

These lamentations reached the ears of a surgeon named Neumant. He hastened to the royal tent, and obtained leave to examine the king's wound. "I assure your Majesty," he said, after carefully looking at it, "that if you will allow me to make some deep incisions, I can save your leg."

"Can you, my man?" replied Charles; "cut away then at once; cut away boldly, and fear nothing." The surgeon did so; and the king, holding his leg between his hands during the operation, looked on as unconcernedly at the incisions made, as if they were made on another person. And while the wound was being dressed, he was giving orders for a fresh attack on Pultowa.

"What an extraordinary man our master is!" said the surgeon Neumant to General Sparre, a few hours after the operation; "nothing dismays him! In this desert country, shut in between two rivers, without food, without artillery, and five hundred leagues from Stockholm, he is going, with twenty thousand men, to attack an army of seventy thousand! And unable to stand, he actually intends to be carried in a litter at the head of his troops!

It appears to me a wild and dangerous resolution."

"It is a little hazardous, certainly," answered the general; "but then think of the successes we have had! think of the difficulties we have already overcome in this barbarous country, and remember our leader is rightly named 'the Invincible.' True, we have but four cannon; but we do not fear the superior numbers of the enemy. It is on the bravery of the soldiers, and the skill of the general, that a victory mainly depends; and who so brave as our hardy Swedes? who such a master of the art of war as Charles the Twelfth?"

"Still you will miss your artillery, general. Think of having left it all in the marshes and rivers, for want of horses to bring it on! What a terrible march that was! In this desolate region, and during such an extremely severe winter, two thousand of our brave troops perishing from cold, and the rest without provisions, without shoes, and almost without clothes, who but Charles would have attempted it? And no news from Sweden could reach us! Do you remember Roos telling the king how much he desired tidings from home? 'What,' said Charles, 'you want to be with your family again? If you are a true soldier, I will take you so far that news from Sweden will scarcely be able to reach you once in three years.'"

General Sparre smiled. "Well, Neumant," he said, "you must allow King Charles shared in all the dangers and fatigue. Do you forget the day, when a river interposing between us and the Russians, he threw himself into the water at the head of his foot-guards, and crossed both river and marsh with the water often up to his shoulders? and having sent his cavalry round, he thus attacked the enemy at once in front and rear."

"I remember it well," said Neumant. "It was in that battle that young Gullenstein was wounded. Charles much loved him; and with a magnanimity not often practiced, insisted on giving up his own horse to him, while he himself remained on foot, at the head of his infantry. After that kind and heroic action, I followed him more cheerfully through the extensive marshes, immense forests, and wild deserts by which he led us. You know, in one of those forests it was necessary to cut down the trees all the way, to make a road for the troops; and in another, fifty leagues in length, and full of swamps, we lost our way!"

"O, he is a brave warrior! Think of the day at Smolensko. Two of his aides-de-camp fell by his side, his horse was killed under him; a groom was presenting him with another, when both groom and horse were shot dead, and then Charles fought on foot with astonishing valor. I was close to him that day, and he killed twelve of the enemy with his own hand!"

"Well," said the surgeon, "I must confess I would rather have cured twelve."

"And then," continued the general, "how his example raised the drooping spirits of the army! You were not with our division, I think, when the following little incident occurred. A soldier one day came before the king, and with much grumbling, showed him a piece of black, moldy bread, made of barley and oats, the only food we then had, and of that there was but a very scanty supply. Charles took the bread, ate it all, and then coolly said, 'It is not very good, but it can be eaten.' Why, Neumant, what we suffered would have been intolerable under any other leader than Charles the Twelfth!"

"Most true, general. When I saw our brave troops crossing the river Desna, in their accustomed manner, some swimming, some on hastily constructed rafts, though the banks of the river were so steep the men were obliged to be let down them with cords,—I thought the Czar Peter might well fear such soldiers, led on by such a king."

"Of course he fears us; who would not? When first we invaded Russia, did he not make some proposals of peace to Charles? to which our king haughtily replied, 'I will treat with the Czar at Moscow.' I have heard, that when the Czar received this answer, he observed, 'My brother Charles affects to play the Alexander, but he will not, I hope, find in me a Darius.' Nothing has withstood our victorious arms hitherto; and I trust, notwithstanding our late misfortunes, we shall, ere long, march as conquerors into the capital city of the Emperor of all the Russias."

"I doubt it," replied the surgeon. "It seems to me we are in rather a perilous situation just now. Would we were all back in Sweden!"

"Well, Count Piper thinks with you, and considers it a wild and dangerous undertaking to risk a battle under our present circumstances. However, he knows it would be useless to attempt to alter the king's resolution; so he only shows by his silence on the subject, that he does not approve of the plan. Charles is not one to take advice."

"No; I hope he will not regret it when too late."

The battle was fought—and the Swedes defeated. Charles lost, in that one day, the fruits of nine years' successful war.

Count Piper and several officers were taken prisoners by the Russians; the king, disdaining to fly, was at length forced to do so by his attached friend, General Poniatowski. Five hundred cavaliers rallied round their sovereign, and—compelled to leave his litter and mount a horse, notwithstanding the extreme pain of his wound—Charles the Twelfth fled from the fatal field of Pultowa.

His military chest, his gold, the rich spoils of Poland, and all the baggage, fell into the hands of the Russians. O, what a blow to the conquering Swede!

During his flight his horse was killed under him; but an officer by his side, severely wounded, gave him up his. Fortunately, Count Piper's carriage was found at a little distance, and in this Charles was placed. He had not himself had a carriage since he left Stockholm. With the utmost haste the fugitives then continued their route to the Borysthenes.

All this time Charles had not spoken a single word. At length he asked, "Where is Count Piper?"

"He is taken prisoner, sire."

"And my generals?"

"Also prisoners."

"Prisoners among the Russians!" said the king, shrugging his shoulders; "come, then, let us go to the Turks." He did not look at all disheartened, notwithstanding the terrible mortification he had experienced; no one who saw him could have suspected for a moment that he was wounded, defeated, and escaping for his life.

As he and his followers continued their hasty flight, the carriage broke down, and Charles was again obliged to mount a horse. To add to their misfortunes, as night came on they lost their way in a wood; the king's horse fell from very weariness, and he, quite worn out with fatigue and pain, threw himself on the ground under a tree, and slept for some hours, with the Russians searching on all sides for him. At length they reached the Borysthenes. But in what a state were these once victorious soldiers! Without provisions—and for two days they had not tasted food; without gunpowder—and the

Russians were in quick pursuit; without a bridge over the broad and rapid river,— and without time to make one! Happily, there were a few boats. Charles and some officers passed over in these, while several hundred cavaliers, trusting to their good horses, braved the danger, and swam across. The foot soldiers who tried to do so were all drowned.

While the King of Sweden thus with difficulty escaped, his brave army was a complete wreck. Those soldiers who had gained so many victories were now obliged to defile before the Russian general, and lay their arms at his feet. The Czar sent numbers of them into the wild and desolate regions of Siberia, where officers and men were alike obliged to work for their dayly bread, and where they pined for their Swedish homes which they were never more to see! Count Piper and the surgeon Neumant escaped this melancholy fate, but they were kept prisoners in St. Petersburgh. The former died in Russia; the latter, to his great joy, after some years returned to Sweden.

And what became of Charles? After a wretched journey of some days he arrived safely at Bender, a town in the Turkish dominions. The Russians pursued him to the last, and took some hundreds of his followers prisoners, just as they were entering Turkey.

The Turks received the fugitive king with the greatest kindness and respect; they pitied his misfortunes and gave him an asylum. He and his attendants were abundantly and magnificently furnished with everything that could contribute to their comfort and convenience. All their wants were supplied in the most liberal manner, and the Turkish Sultan generously allowed Charles five hundred crowns a day.

The king recovered from his wound, but he was far from happy. His glory had been tarnished, and the constant restless desire of his heart was to wipe out the stain. In order to accomplish this, he used every art to induce the Sultan to assist him against the Russians. Could he only dethrone Peter the Great, he thought he should be satisfied.

The Turkish Sultan, however, had no wish to enter on a war with Russia. He did not desire to embroil himself with his powerful neighbor. So he sent Charles a present of twenty-five Arabian horses, one of which was covered with a saddle and trappings ornamented with precious stones, and furnished with stirrups of solid gold, and told him he could not give him an army to invade Russia. Soon afterward, he presented the king with five hundred purses, each containing eight hundred crowns, earnestly advising him, at the same time, to return peaceably to his own dominions. This, however, Charles obstinately refused to do.

The Sultan, who resided at Constantinople, had not seen his royal visitor, who lived at Bender, but he heard a good deal of him; and his ministers heard of him too, and began to fear, from his bold and restless spirit, that he would prove rather troublesome. One of them, thinking the allowance granted him was rather too liberal, gave orders to retrench it. It was, as I told you, very large, and far more than necessary to keep him and his court in luxury and abundance. When Charles heard of this order he was highly indignant; he could not brook the slightest want of respect. Turning to the steward of his household, he said, sternly, "Hitherto you have provided only two tables; from this day you will provide four." The steward, not daring to dispute his master's will, was forced to obey, but he had some difficulty in doing so; for Charles was so lavish with his money, and made such liberal presents to his officers, that it was soon gone. However, by borrowing from some merchants, the necessary sum was raised.

And yet, though the King of Sweden did not find the generous allowance granted him sufficient for his expenses, he was himself remarkably abstemious, and averse to luxury. Wine he never tasted; he ate of the plainest food, and always dressed in the simplest style. When in Saxony, he rose at four o'clock, took long rides two or three times a day, required no attendants when dressing, remained at the dinner-table only a quarter of an hour, and knew no other pleasure than that of making Europe tremble. His habits were still the same, and the one desire of his heart was still for glory.

Restless and dissatisfied, Charles continued to solicit the Sultan for a large army that he might invade Russia. But the Sultan could not consent to make an unjust war, and becoming rather wearied of the subject, he wrote a polite letter to his illustrious visitor, requesting his departure. At the same time he promised to furnish him with money, horses, chariots, and everything necessary, and to send with him an escort of eight thousand men to convey him safely into Poland.

The king read the letter, and hoped still to prevail on Sultan Achmet to make war. He wrote back an answer to say "that he should always be grateful to him for the favors he had received, but that he could not go with so small an escort into Poland, as the Russian troops were there." The Sultan was not aware of this; but he at once made an agreement with the Czar that his soldiers should leave Poland, and the King of Sweden be permitted to pass through that country without the slightest molestation.

But Charles was obstinate still. Instead of wishing to return to his kingdom, from which he had been so long absent, he only thought of recovering his former glory. So he told the Pacha, or governor of Bender, that he could not go till he had paid his debts, and that he had no money to do so. "How much money does your majesty require?" asked the Pacha, rather surprised that Charles had not found his large allowance sufficient for him. "O, about a thousand purses," replied the king carelessly. Pacha Ismael wrote to Constantinople, and the Sultan, instead of a thousand, generously sent twelve hundred purses, expressly commanding the governor, at the same time, not to deliver them to the king till the very moment of his departure.*

---

* Each purse contained thirty sequins. A sequin is a gold coin worth about two dollars; consequently the twelve hundred purses contained seventy-two thousand dollars.

Charles's treasurer, however, managed to get the money, saying, "they really must have it to make preparations for the journey."

"We will see to that," replied Ismael; "as long as you are in Turkey, your expenses shall be paid."

"Ah, but our carriages are made in such a different way to yours," said the treasurer, "we must give orders about them. We shall soon be ready to go, but I must have the money now."

Pacha Ismael reluctantly gave up the money; but on going a few days afterward to visit Charles, and receive his last orders, he heard him say, to his extreme surprise, "that he was not going to leave Turkey yet, and that before he did set out, he must have a thousand purses more!"

The truth was, that Charles, indignant at being, in a manner, *ordered* out of the Turkish dominions, had just made up his mind not to go at all!

When the Pacha heard the king's answer, it was some minutes before he could speak. At length, with tears in his eyes, he said, "I shall lose my head for having obliged your majesty. I gave you the twelve hundred purses contrary to my sovereign's orders." He was taking leave with a sorrowful countenance, when Charles stopped him: "O," he said, "I will excuse you to the Sultan; I will explain it all; fear not." "Ah!" replied Ismael, as he went away, "my master does not know how to excuse faults; he only knows how to punish them."

The Pacha wrote to the Sultan an account of what had passed. Charles also wrote, asking for a thousand purses more. It was not covetousness, so much as extravagance, which made him do this. Extremely generous, indeed lavish of money himself, he seemed to think nothing of his large demands on the generosity of another. The Sultan was highly indignant. He threw the king's messenger into prison, acquitted Pacha Ismael of blame, and at once assembled an extraordinary divan or council of state.

Sultan Achmet then, his eyes flashing

with indignation, made a speech to the members,—a thing of rare occurrence with him. "I scarcely knew the king of Sweden," he said, "except by his defeat at Pultowa, and the request he made to me for an asylum in my dominions. I have not, I believe, any need of his assistance, nor any cause to love or fear him. Nevertheless, I have received, protected, and maintained him, his ministers, officers, and soldiers, according to the dignity of a king; and for the space of three years and a half have continued to load him with favors. I have granted him a considerable guard to conduct him back to his own kingdom. He asked for a thousand purses to pay some debts, though I defray all his expenses; instead of a thousand I granted him twelve hundred; and having received these, he yet refuses to depart until he shall obtain a thousand more, and a stronger guard, although that already appointed is more than sufficient! I ask you, therefore, whether it will be a breach of the laws of hospitality to send away this prince, or whether foreign powers can reasonably tax me with cruelty or injustice if I use force to hasten his departure?"

All the members of the Divan answered that such conduct would be consistent with strict justice.

An order was then sent to the Pacha of Bender to compel Charles to leave Turkey; and if he would not go with fair words, force must be used.

Ismael accordingly went to the king, and told him of the order he had received. Charles was most indignant. "Obey your master if you dare!" he exclaimed; "and leave me instantly!"

The Pacha did not need this insult to animate him to do his duty. He calmly prepared to obey his sovereign's commands, and at once desired that no more provisions should be taken to the Swedish camp.

"I do not want their provisions or their presents either!" exclaimed King Charles angrily; "go instantly and shoot twenty of the Arabian horses they sent me." No one dared to expostulate; and the beautiful creatures were all shot dead in the meadow.

Charles then prepared to defend himself; and with his three hundred Swedish soldiers, and his attendants, coolly determined to resist a large army of Turks and Tartars. He threw up entrenchments round the camp, and he, his ministers, his soldiers, and all his servants, labored diligently in the work. They then barricaded the house; and when every door and window seemed secure, Charles composedly sat down to a game of chess with his treasurer. But down came the Turks with ten cannon! They forced the intrenchments, and took the three hundred Swedish soldiers prisoners in a very short time. Charles, who was then on horseback between the camp and his house, cried out, "Let us defend the house!" and, galloping back, found that more than a hundred and fifty Turks had entered by a window. They were in possession of all the apartments, except the large hall, to which the servants had retired. The king leaped from his horse, sword in hand, and killed or wounded all who opposed him. A Turk aimed a musket at him; the ball grazed his nose, and carried off part of his ear; but he heeded it not, and forced his way into the house. The servants then opened the hall door, delighted to see their master safe. But inactivity did not suit Charles. "Here are sixty of us," he exclaimed, looking round; "come, we will chase these barbarians out of my house,—there are not two hundred of them." And, opening the door, he rushed out at the head of his followers, chased the Turks from room to room, and soon cleared the house; for, from respect to the king's person, and from surprise at his sudden onset, the Turks made little opposition, but jumped out of the window as fast as they had jumped in. Charles found two of them under his bed; he killed one, but the other cried for mercy.

"I grant it," said the king, "on condition that you go and tell the Pacha what you have seen."

The man gladly promised this, and was permitted to jump from the window after his companions.

The Swedes having firmly barricaded the house, fired from the windows on the Turks, and in a quarter of an hour killed more than two hundred of them. It was grievous, indeed, that the obstinacy of the Swedish king should be the cause of such carnage. His friends had before,—seeing the folly of opposing, with his small band, an army of twenty thousand Turks, entreated him not to risk his life, and the lives of his followers, in the attempt.

"Go and tell the Turks," he said, "if they intend to attack us, we are ready to defend ourselves. I do not want advice from any one."

The cannon balls battered the house in vain. But ere long the Swedes perceived that they were in great danger. The Turks, by shooting up lighted arrows into the roof, had set the house on fire, and half of the roof fell in! Amidst the noise and the smoke, the voice of the king was heard. "Let us extinguish the fire," he said; and, taking up a barrel, with the assistance of two officers, he threw it on the burning mass. They supposed it was a barrel of water, but it contained spirits, and the flames burnt more fiercely and brilliantly than before.

"We must surrender now," said a sentinel.

"Here is a strange fellow," observed Charles; "he thinks it is better to be made prisoner, than to be burnt alive with his king!"

"Your majesty," said another sentinel, already wounded, "the chancellor's house has a stone roof, and is fire-proof:—let us go forth, take possession of that, and defend it to the last."

"There is a true Swede!" exclaimed the king. "My friend, I promote you to the rank of colonel for the brave thought. Come on, then, and let us take all the powder and ball we can carry."

A sword in one hand, and a pistol in the other, Charles furiously sallied forth, at the head of his little band. The Turks beheld with amazement, not unmixed with admiration, the desperate onset of the intrepid Swedes, so few in number. The moment they appeared at the door, each man gave two cuts with his sword, and fired off his musket. Taken by surprise, the Turks retreated at least fifty feet; but soon recovering themselves, they surrounded and overpowered the little troop. Charles, being in his boots, as usual, entangled himself with his spurs, and fell. One-and-twenty soldiers sprang upon him; he threw his sword up into the air, to avoid the mortification of surrendering it; and some of the soldiers taking hold of his legs, and some of his arms, he was carried in that manner to the tent of the Pacha!

You may believe Charles did not feel very glorious now. He acted so strangely in this affair, and at other times during his life, that he has been styled "the illustrious madman."

He was an extraordinary man. From the moment he was thus seized by the soldiers, the violence and fury which had urged him on in the desperate combat ceased, and gave place at once to mildness and composure. Not a glance of anger,—not a single word of impatience escaped him;

he even smiled at the men who bore him along in so unkingly a style. The Turks regarded him with mingled feelings of respect and indignation.

When the Pacha entered the tent, he saluted Charles gravely and respectfully, to which, however, the king gave no heed.

"I regret extremely," said Ismael, "that your majesty has compelled me to execute the orders of my master. Let me entreat you now to take some repose on a sofa; and consider all in my house as entirely at your service."

Charles, however, remained standing. "The only thing I regret," he said, "is that my three hundred Swedes allowed themselves to be taken prisoners. Had they defended their post as they ought to have done, the camp would not have been forced these ten days."

The Pacha Ismael treated Charles as a king, gave him up his own apartments, and behaved in a kind and hospitable manner. He took care, nevertheless, to place a strong guard at the door of his room. A friend coming to visit and condole with the king, found him lying on a sofa, his clothes torn, his boots, hands, and dress covered with blood and powder, his eyebrows burnt, and part of his ear gone; but with a perfectly serene air.

"Well, what did you think of the famous battle of Bender?" said Charles, laughing.

"Why, they say your majesty killed twenty Turks with your own hand!"

"Capital!" replied the king; "they always exaggerate these things one-half."

The next day, the Pacha conducted Charles toward Adrianople, as a captive, in a chariot covered with scarlet. The officers who accompanied their king, could not refrain from tears every time they looked at the carriage. One of them entreated the Pacha to return King Charles his sword. "Not on any account!" replied Ismael; "he would cut off all our beards!"

He, however, restored it a short time afterward.

The sultan allowed his royal captive to reside at Demotica, a small town about eighteen miles from Adrianople. Here he was supplied with provisions for himself and his household; but only twenty-five crowns a day were granted him, instead of the five hundred he had received at Bender. But fearing that now he was a prisoner he might not be treated with proper respect by the Turks who should see him, he took the extraordinary resolution of keeping his bed, under pretense of sickness; and this he actually did for ten months!

In the mean time, what had happened? While Charles, from his unreasonable pride, remained so long in the Turkish dominions, and even kept his bed, for fear of the slightest want of respect to his greatness, Sweden was in a very distressed state indeed. Russia, Poland, and Denmark, taking advantage of the absence of her king, all made war upon her, and stripped her of her possessions. Stanislaus was also deposed, and taken prisoner; and Augustus once more sat on the throne of Poland.

Hearing of the troubled state of his kingdom, and of the change in Polish affairs, and despairing of making the Turks take arms in his favor, Charles at last told the sultan he was ready to return home. Achmet and his ministers were equally ready to part with him. They furnished him with everything necessary for the journey, loaded sixty wagons with provisions for him by the way, and gave him an escort of three hundred horse. But they gave him no money this time. The king's treasurer tried to borrow some from the sultan, but his chief minister replied, "that his master knew how to *give*, when he thought proper; but it was beneath his dignity to *lend*."

Before he set out, Charles sent his ministers with great pomp to take leave of the sultan for him; and you may believe Achmet was not sorry to bid farewell to his troublesome visitor, who had now been in Turkey more than five years!

On the 14th of October, 1714, Charles left his bed at Demotica, and set out for Sweden. As soon as he had really started, the hospitable and generous sultan sent him a present of a large scarlet tent, embroidered with gold, a saber garnished with precious stones, and eight Arabian horses, of perfect beauty, with superb saddles, and stirrups of solid silver.

In order to show respect to the King of Sweden, the Turks traveled but a short distance each day. This slow manner of proceeding, however, did not at all suit the impatient Charles, so he resolved to alter it. Rising every morning at three o'clock, as soon as he was dressed, he awoke the officers and soldiers himself, and ordered all to march, in the middle of the dark night! The grave Turks were quite disturbed by this new mode of journeying; but Charles only laughed at their embarrassment, and said,—"I am but taking a little revenge for the Bender affair."

As he approached the frontiers of Turkey, he heard that all the princes through whose territories he was to pass had given orders for his entertainment in the most magnificent manner. Towns and villages were making preparations to receive him;—all wished to catch a glimpse of the extraordinary man whose victories and misfortunes had made so much noise both in Europe and Asia. "I shall, then, disappoint them," said Charles; "I have no inclination to go through the fatigue of all their pomp and ceremony; or to show myself off as the prisoner of Bender."

So, at Targoivity, on the borders of Transylvania, after dismissing his Turkish escort, he assembled all his followers in a large barn, and said to them,—"Now do not trouble yourselves any more about me, my friends, but make the best of your way, with all speed, to Stralsund, on the coast of the Baltic; it is but fifteen hundred miles from hence: you will find me there. Rosen and During, I desire your attendance alone."

In high spirits, he took leave of his suit, while they, overwhelmed with surprise and sorrow, saw him depart with fear and consternation. To disguise himself, Charles put on a black wig, and took the name of a German officer. Avoiding, as much as he could, the territories of those who were hostile to him, he traversed nearly all Germany, and thus went so much out of his way as to lengthen his journey extremely. With the greatest possible haste, he hurried on; by day on horseback, and by night in a carriage, taking food and rest as he could, without stopping anywhere. At the close of the first day's journey, young During, not able to bear such excessive fatigue, fainted in alighting from his horse, and was obliged to remain at an inn on the road.

After sixteen days of incessant traveling, Charles reached Stralsund, in the middle of the night.

"Go," said the king to the sentinel at the gates, "inform the governor, General Ducker, that a courier from the King of Sweden desires to speak with him."

"The governor is in bed," replied the soldier: "it is too late to speak with him to-night. You must wait till to-morrow morning."

"I will not wait!" said the king; "I am come on very important business; and if you do not awake the governor at once, you shall be well punished to-morrow."

The soldier then sent a message to the governor, who was asleep. The message only half awakened him; but he desired that the courier should be admitted. When Charles entered the room, General Ducker, scarcely opening his eyes, said,—"Any news from the King of Sweden?"

"What, Ducker!" exclaimed the king, "have my most faithful subjects forgotten me?"

At the sound of his voice, the general recognized his master; he sprang out of bed, threw himself at the king's feet, and shed tears of joy. The news of Charles's arrival spread through the town; every one rose from bed; the soldiers surrounded the governor's house, and the streets were soon crowded with people, who eagerly inquired one from another,—"Is it true that the king is come?"

On finding it was indeed true, all the houses were illuminated; and the light of a thousand flambeaux, with the thunder of artillery, proved that he was a welcome visitor.

Charles, as you may suppose, was somewhat fatigued with his long journey; he had not lain down for sixteen days, and they were obliged to cut his boots off, his feet were so swollen. But he only took a few hours' repose, and then rose to review his troops, and visit the fortifications. The same day, this extraordinary monarch sent forth his orders that fiercer war than ever should be recommenced with all his enemies!

Not long after this, Stralsund was besieged by the Danes and Prussians. During this siege, Charles performed prodigies of valor; and, as usual, feared nothing. One day, as he was dictating some letters to his secretary, a bomb fell upon the house, passed through the roof, and burst, with a loud explosion, near the room in which the king was. The bombs were falling on the houses as thick as hail, and half the town was in ashes. At the noise of the bomb, and the falling in of part of the house, the terrified secretary let fall his pen.

"Well, what is the matter?" said Charles: "why do you not go on writing?"

"Ah, sire! the bomb, the bomb!" was all that the frightened secretary could say.

"Well," said the king, quietly, "what

has the bomb to do with that letter? Go on."

I must give you one more scene in the life of Charles the Twelfth, ere I conclude my story.

In 1718, he was in Norway, with the hope of conquering that kingdom. It was in the month of December, and he was besieging the strong and important town of Frederickshall. The cold was so intense that the soldiers frequently fell down dead at their posts; and the severity of the frost rendered it almost impossible to break the ground. Charles, however, resolved to form trenches; and the men cheerfully obeyed, digging into the ground with as much labor as though they were piercing a rock. Indeed, they could not complain, with the example of their royal master before them. He slept at night in his cloak, on straw, in the open field, and exposed himself to the same hardships as the meanest soldier. Wishing to see how long he could remain without food, he, for five days, neither ate nor drank anything; and then, taking a long ride one morning before breakfast, he made a very hearty meal, without his health being in the slightest degree injured by the experiment.

But notwithstanding this iron constitution, and this bold, determined will, Charles of Sweden fell a victim to his love of glory. He braved danger once too often. One night, during the siege, he went out to inspect the trenches. As he was watching the men digging by the light of the stars, leaning with his elbows on the parapet, in the midst of a terrible fire from the enemy, a ball entered his right temple, and he immediately expired without a groan.

Thus died Charles the Twelfth of Sweden, at the age of thirty-six. With many great qualities, he had equally great faults. He lived for his own glory, not for the good of his subjects. Dazzling as his career was, his country derived no benefit from it, for he left it in a miserable condition, drained of men and money. He was a very different character from his great ancestor, Gustavus Adolphus. Of him it has been said,—

"His ashes in a peaceful urn shall rest:
  His name a great example stands, to show
How strangely high endeavors may be blest,
  Where piety and valor jointly go."

But Charles the Twelfth had no religion to guide him; though he had an iron constitution and an iron will.

"His fall was destined to a barren strand,
A petty fortress, and a dubious hand;
He left a name at which the world grew pale,
To point a moral, or adorn a tale."

Fall of the Hats and the Caps.

On the morning of the 19th of August, 1772, a small family party was assembled at breakfast in one of the best houses in Stockholm. It consisted of a young officer named Captain Frederic Cederstrom, his mother, and his little sister Olga. The latter was pouring out the coffee, and as she handed a cup to her brother, she observed, smilingly, "You are going out in all your magnificence to-day, Captain Frederic; is anything particular to take place?"

"Not that I know of, little Olga," replied her brother. "The king has summoned a considerable number of officers to attend him early this morning, and myself among them. Your coffee is excellent, Olga; you will be a good housekeeper one of these days, after all."

"Let me fill your cup again," said the little girl, pleased with her brother's appro-

KING GUSTAVUS AND HIS OFFICERS.

See page 170

bation; for to be a good housekeeper was her great desire. "Perhaps, Frederic, the king is going to make you a colonel?"

"Or a general, Olga. You would have to treat me with great respect then."

Olga laughed merrily. "I am sure the king must be very proud of such a fine young officer," she said; "in such a splendid dress, too, and with such a great sword! Do you like his majesty, Fred?"

"Certainly; King Gustavus has always been most kind to me. He is very affable, too; I think I must ask him to honor this house with his presence some day, that I may introduce to him my saucy little sister."

"Do all the officers like him, Frederic?"

"Yes; though Gustavus the Third has only been on the throne a year, he has won our esteem and love. We know him to be brave, heroic, enterprising, and merciful; and such qualities must win a soldier's heart."

"And what a liberal and enlightened patron he is of the arts and sciences, my son," said Madame Cederstrom; "the men of learning are delighted with him. Sweden has had two great kings of the name of Gustavus; I hope she will have a third to equal them."

"He gives promise, dear mother, of being all Sweden could wish; but he is not in the position exactly of either Gustavus Vasa, or Gustavus Adolphus. The first reigned with great power; and for the second the States would do anything, he was so beloved. But since the death of Charles the Twelfth, the whole power of the kingdom has been lodged in the States, and our present king is one of the most limited monarchs in Europe."

"Then he cannot do much without the permission of the States?" asked Olga.

"Scarcely anything. On some occasions the States have grievously abused their power; and it appears to me that King Gustavus does not approve of being a king in name only. I should not be much surprised if we had a change before long."

"What was that oath you took at the senate-house the other day, brother?"

"I took an oath to be faithful to the States, Olga. It is my duty to obey the government of my country."

"But should you not like King Gustavus to have more power?"

"I should, certainly, as I think he would make a good use of it. Still, a soldier must take a soldier's oath to fight for his country, and obey her established laws."

"In England they have king, lords, and commons to make the laws of the land; have they not, Fred?"

"They have; thus the sovereign, the nobility, and the people, have a share in the government, and each party is a check upon the other. Free and happy England! her people are protected, and her laws are just, impartial, and merciful."

"I want to ask you a question, Frederic," said Olga. "Will you tell me what is meant by the Hats and Caps, for I cannot make out? Uncle Magnus says he is a Hat, and cousin Charles calls himself a Cap; and the other day, when I went to play with the little Franks, they said, 'Let us play at Hats and Caps.' I did not know what that meant; but we played, and I saw we were divided into two opposing parties."

"Ah, Gustaf Frank is a Hat, and a violent one, so I suppose his children know something of the dispute between the factions. The *Hats*, as they are termed, are those who would uphold a constitutional monarchy; the *Caps*, those who would increase the power of the people at the expense of the crown. Our Hats and Caps are much the same as the Tories and Whigs in England."

"Then I should belong to the Hats, certainly," said Olga, laughingly. "Look, Fred, there is your prancing steed at the door, all impatience to be gone. I do think something must be going to happen, as you are sent for so early."

"Do not puzzle your little head about it," said the young officer, as he rose from the table. "I would advise you to attend to your knitting, or the trimming of your bonnet, and not decide yet whether you will be a Hat or a Cap, Olga."

So saying, and taking an affectionate

leave of his mother and sister, Captain Cederstrom vaulted into his saddle and galloped off. Olga watched him till he was out of sight, and then began busily to employ herself under her mother's direction.

Cederstrom, proceeding to the palace, found the king already on horseback, and about to visit his artillery regiment. He and a few other officers accompanied him, and as they rode through the streets, Frederic could not but observe that Gustavus was more than usually courteous to all he met, bowing familiarly to the very lowest of the people. On their return to the palace, the detachment which was to mount guard that day being drawn up, together with that which was to be relieved, the king retired with all the officers into the guard-room. Cederstrom saw, by a glance at the monarch's countenance, that something important was about to take place. It was so. Gustavus the Third, determined to abridge the power of the States—determined to be a king in reality, and not in name only—resolved that day to effect a revolution in Sweden. With all that eloquence of which he is said to have been a perfect master, he addressed the assembled officers; he exposed to them in the strongest colors the wretched state of the kingdom, and the dissensions and troubles with which it abounded. "My only design," he continued, "is to put an end to these troubles, to banish corruption, restore true liberty, and revive the ancient luster of the Swedish name. Be assured that I disclaim forever absolute monarchy; but I am obliged to defend my own liberty, and that of the kingdom, against the aristocracy which reigns. Will you, gentlemen, be faithful to me, as your forefathers were to Gustavus Vasa and Gustavus Adolphus? I will then risk my life for your welfare and that of my country."

"We will! we will!" cried the officers, who were most of them young men, and thoroughly attached to the king. "We will be faithful to your majesty, even to death itself!"

They then, pressing eagerly forward, took an oath of fidelity to their sovereign.

Three, however, in that assembly stood still, and one of these was Frederic Cederstrom.

"How is this, Cederstrom?" said the king; "do you not take the oath of fealty to your lawful sovereign?"

"I regret that I cannot take that oath," said the young officer with respect; "your majesty has not a more faithful subject in Sweden than myself; but I have already and very lately taken an oath to be faithful to the States, and consequently I cannot take that which your majesty now requires from me."

"Think of what you are saying, Captain Cederstrom," said King Gustavus sternly.

"I do, your majesty," replied Frederic, "and what I think to-day I shall think to-morrow; and were I capable of breaking the oath by which I am already bound to the States, I should be likewise capable of breaking that your majesty now requests me to take."

"This is conduct I should scarcely have expected from one of the captains of my guard," said the king; "you are in arrest, sir! deliver up your sword."

Cederstrom obeyed. As the high-spirited young officer retired to the further end of the guard-room, many friendly looks followed him; for his kind, conciliating manners, and his uniformly firm and courageous conduct, joined to a strict regard for truth, had gained him the love and esteem of all his associates.

"Fred Cederstrom never broke his word yet," whispered one officer to another, "and he will not do it now; though the love and reverence he bears the king are such, that I will venture to say at this moment, he is longing to place himself at the head of his guards, take possession of the senate-house, execute all his majesty's orders with courage and fidelity, and even die for him if necessary. There is not a braver or more faithful heart in Sweden! But see, the king speaks."

Gustavus then ordered that two regiments of guards and of artillery should be immediately assembled; and that a detachment of thirty-six grenadiers should be posted at the door of the council-chamber, to prevent any of the senators from coming out.

While these instructions were being given, the king occasionally glanced toward Cederstrom with a troubled look; and at length, a question arising as to who should fill that officer's place at the head of his troop, Gustavus replied, "Captain Cederstrom shall settle that point himself. I beg your attendance here, sir."

Frederic advanced from the end of the room, where he had been standing, and respectfully awaited his sovereign's commands. There was not the slightest shade of anger on his countenance; and as the king looked on his ingenuous features, modest and truthful, he felt that there were few in the army he could trust as he could him.

"Captain Cederstrom," said Gustavus in a firm yet mild voice, "you have ever stood high in my esteem, and what has now passed has not lowered you in it. I respect your love of truth and honor; and as a proof of the opinion I entertain of you, and the confidence I place in you, I return you your sword, without insisting on your taking the oath. I can trust you; and I only desire your attendance this day."

Frederic was touched by the king's kindness. The tears rose in his eyes, but he remained firm. "Sire," he replied, as he fell on his knees before his royal master, "I am not insensible to your goodness. I rejoice that I have not fallen in your opinion. Believe me, your majesty has not in the army a soldier more devoted to your service, or one more ready to risk his life in your cause. But I took that oath of fidelity to the States calmly and deliberately, and I cannot calmly and deliberately break it. Whatever success I may wish your majesty, I must beg you to excuse my attendance to-day."

"Be it so," said Gustavus, looking half-vexed, and yet not displeased at the firmness and integrity his young officer evinced; "be it so, Cederstrom; I trust by to-morrow you will be more willing to serve your king. Now, gentlemen, obey your orders."

Before the orders could be carried into

execution, however, it was necessary that the king should address himself to the soldiers; men in utter ignorance of his designs, and accustomed to pay obedience only to the orders of the senate, whom they had been taught to hold in the highest reverence.

As Gustavus, followed by the officers, was advancing from the guard-room to the parade for this purpose, some of them, more cautious, or perhaps more timid than the rest, became, on a short reflection, rather fearful of the consequences of the measure in which they were engaged. They expressed their apprehensions to the king. "Unless some persons of greater weight and influence than ourselves take a part in the same cause, we almost fear your majesty will not succeed in your enterprise," they said.

"Do you think so?" said the king, stopping, and appearing to hesitate.

"It *shall* succeed!" cried a serjeant of the guards, who had overheard the conversation; "it shall succeed—long live Gustavus the Third!"

"Then I will venture," said the king; and stepping forward to the soldiers, he addressed them in terms nearly similar to those he had made use of to the officers, and with the same success. They answered him with repeated acclamations; and long and loud were the shouts of "Long live Gustavus the Third!" "Long life to our patriot king!"

In the mean time a report had spread through the town that the king was arrested. On hearing this, the people ran in great numbers to the palace, where they arrived just as Gustavus had concluded his address to the guards. They testified by reiterated shouts their joy at seeing him safe; a joy which promised the happiest conclusion to the business of the day.

The senators were now immediately secured. They had, from the window of the council-chamber, seen all that was going forward on the parade before the palace, and wondering what the king could be saying to the soldiers, and what all the shouting was about, determined to inquire. On descending the stairs for this purpose, they were stopped by thirty grenadiers, who informed them, it was his majesty's pleasure they should continue where they were.

"What does this mean?" exclaimed the indignant senators; "what is this insult to the States of Sweden?—let us pass instantly, or both you and your master will have cause to repent it!"

The soldiers made no other reply to this speech, than by shutting the door and locking it.

The moment the secret committee heard that the senate was arrested, they separated in alarm, each individual providing for his own safety.

The king then mounted his horse, and followed by his officers with their swords drawn, a large body of soldiers, and a great crowd of people, went to the other quarters of the town, where the soldiers he had ordered to be assembled were posted. He found them all equally ready to support his cause, and to take an oath of fidelity to him.

As Gustavus passed thus through the

streets of his capital, and beheld the wondering countenances of his people, he said to them in a firm yet kind tone, "My faithful subjects, you may wonder at the events of to-day; believe me, when I say, I mean only to defend you, and save my country from ruin. If you are unwilling to confide in the word of your king, he will at once lay down his sceptre, and surrender up his kingdom."

So much was Gustavus beloved by the people, that on hearing these words, there arose from them renewed shouts of "Long live the king!" "Long live Gustavus!" while many of them fell down upon their knees, and, with tears in their eyes, implored their sovereign not to abandon them.

Little Olga Cederstrom had been obliged to lay down her knitting at the noise and shouting she heard. "See, mamma!" she exclaimed, on going to the window; "the king is passing with all his officers, and such a crowd of people! what can be the matter? The officers have their swords drawn, and they look so pleased. But I do not see Frederic,—where can he be?"

"Perhaps his majesty has dispatched him on some message, my love. How pleased the people seem to be! I think there must be some great cause for joy; I will send out Anderson to see what it is."

"It may have been a battle between the Hats and the Caps," said Olga, smiling, "in which both parties were defeated. I have heard Fred say, neither king nor people like them."

In the mean time, Gustavus proceeded on his way; and in less than an hour made himself master of all the military force in Stockholm. During his progress through the city, the heralds, by proclamation, summoned an assembly of the States for the ensuing morning, and declared all members who should not appear to be traitors to their country.

"O, Frederic! I am so glad you are come!" exclaimed Olga, as her brother entered the room; "now you can tell us what is the matter to-day in Stockholm. We have heard such strange reports. Some say there has been a revolution; others say the senators are all in prison; and one told us—but *that* I cannot believe—that—that you had been placed in arrest, and obliged to deliver up your sword to the king!"

"The senators were only confined for a short time, and are now at liberty," replied Frederic; "the other reports you heard were true, Olga."

"Brother!" said the little girl, in astonishment, "you cannot mean that you were placed under arrest by the king's command?"

"Even so, Olga."

"But here is your sword?"

"His majesty returned it to me."

"O, do tell me all about it, Fred; I cannot believe you are in disgrace with the king, because, though you are trying to look grave, I can see a smile now and then which shows me that in reality you are pleased at something."

Frederic laughed. "Well, Olga, since you have discovered so much," he said, "I will tell you as a secret, that I *am* pleased. There has been a great revolution to-day."

"A revolution!"

"Yes, but it is not yet completed; you will hear more of it to-morrow."

"I hope no one has been killed, Frederic?"

"No one; it has been a perfectly peaceful, though a very surprising day."

Frederic then told his sister what had happened.

"And do you think King Gustavus is angry with you because you would not break your word?" said Olga.

"I can answer that question better to-morrow," said her brother. "I shall be on duty at the palace as usual."

The night passed very tranquilly. Not a murmur was expressed, not a disturbance was raised. On the morrow Gustavus repaired, in all the pomp of royalty, surrounded by his guards, to the assembly of the States. Nearly the whole population of Stockholm crowded to the palace. Holding in his hand the silver scepter of Gustavus Adolphus, the king addressed his people. He was the first monarch since Charles the Twelfth that could speak to them in the national language, and his speech was listened to with loud applause. He lamented the state of the country, and reproached the States for their abuse of power. Conviction, or fear, kept the senators silent. They knew they had done wrong; they knew they had been bribed with foreign gold, and sacrificed the welfare of Sweden to their own ambition. The secretary then read the new form of government, which the king submitted to the approbation of the States. When he asked them if they approved of it, they answered him by loud acclamations. The Hats exulted in the downfall of their rivals; the Caps huzzaed as loudly as if the revolution had been their own work. Not one in that large assembly refused to sign the articles of the new constitution. And the king returned to his palace amidst the enthusiastic shouts of his people.

"The most remarkable feature in this extraordinary revolution," said Frederic Cederstrom, as he conversed with his mother and sister, on his return home, "is that it has been begun and perfected without the slightest bloodshed. And in twenty-four hours too! All parties seem to rejoice in the change; all are talking of the wisdom, firmness, and courage of our king."

"Then it will be a good thing for Sweden?" asked Olga.

"Certainly. The States have greatly abused their power, and the people are much dissatisfied with them. The monarchy is now absolute; that is, the same powers are granted to Gustavus which belonged to the ancient kings of Sweden."

"But what do the Hats and Caps say to the revolution, brother?"

"They appear to be equally pleased with it. The king, however, has issued a proclamation, that those terms, which serve to designate the hostile parties, shall not be used in future, as they only keep up a spirit of enmity. There are to be no more Hats and Caps, my little Olga."

"O! then we must not play with the Franks at that game any more, I suppose?"

"Of course not," said Frederic, gravely; "you must play at something else now."

"Well, I do not quite understand about

the Hats and Caps, and what harm they did," said Olga.

"The party of the Hats, Olga, is liked and supported by France, and the party of the Caps by Russia, so that when those two powers are hostile to each other, Stockholm is the place where they struggle for the ascendency by the influence of gold, and adherents to their cause. You can understand that this must be a bad thing for Sweden. Besides, factions jealous of each other, as the Hats and Caps are, must do harm in a country."

"Then now that there is a new form of government, I suppose you may take the oath of allegiance to the king, without breaking your oath to the States?"

"I have done so, Olga, already. When the States swore to support the new constitution, I was among the first to vow allegiance to my sovereign. I can now obey all his commands with joy, fidelity, and honor."

"I am glad of that, Fred, for the Bible tells us to honor and obey the king, you know. Did he speak to you?"

"He did, and invited me to a grand banquet he gives at the palace to-day. It is time I should prepare for it."

The banquet was a magnificent one, and King Gustavus charmed all his guests by his kind and condescending manner. He had great powers of conversation, a cultivated mind, and fine talents. Whether talking to the man of science, or the man of literature, the noble or the soldier, all were equally delighted with him, and all felt proud of their sovereign.

As Frederic Cederstrom stood among a group of officers, talking of the events of the day, Gustavus approached, and joined in the conversation. After congratulating his officers on the peaceful revolution they had effected, he observed, looking at Cederstrom, "There was, however, one of you, gentlemen, unwilling yesterday to draw sword in his sovereign's cause. Such an example is not good for the army, is it, think you?"

"My liege," said young Cederstrom, modestly, yet firmly, "being absolved from my oath to the States by the great events which have taken place, I have this day sworn allegiance to your majesty. My life is at your service, and I rejoice that I can obey all your commands from henceforth with a free conscience and a glad will. I trust your majesty will graciously pardon the *appearance* of disloyalty in a true and faithful subject."

"Pardon you, Cederstrom!" said the king, "can you expect it? I honor you, my brave officer, I honor you for your stern integrity and true fidelity, though it was well for me that all did not act as you did," continued Gustavus, smiling, "or we should not be standing here now. Your conduct of yesterday gives me the fullest assurance that you will well and faithfully serve your king; and to show the confidence I place in you, I promote you to the rank of colonel."

A murmur of applause ran round the circle of brave officers at the king's speech; much as they had always loved and esteemed their sovereign, their respect and affection for him this evening, aided by the events of the last two days, was increased tenfold.

Gustavus made a good use of the power he had obtained. He took care that the law should be administered with strict impartiality to the richest noble and to the poorest peasant, making a severe example of such judges as were proved to have taken bribes. He gave particular attention and encouragement to commerce, was a liberal and enlightened patron of learning and science, and endeavored to introduce into his kingdom the most valuable improvements in agriculture that had been made in foreign countries.

While thus active in promoting the arts of peace, he was not inattentive to those of war. He reformed his army and navy, and in a war which he had with Russia, displayed astonishing activity, great military skill, and undaunted courage. But alas! he had one great fault: he was artful, and did not pay a strict regard to truth. To gain his own ends, he had recourse to deceit and falsehood.

Twenty years had passed away since the day of the revolution. On the evening of the 16th of March, 1792, there was a grand masked ball given in Stockholm. As Olga Cederstrom, no longer *little* Olga, sat in her pleasant room reading, the numerous carriages rolling along the street, filled with elegantly dressed ladies, and attended by smart footmen with lighted flambeaux, gave evidence that the ball would be a large one. Olga had declined going to it; she had no wish to leave her happy home, and she preferred a quiet evening with her books to all the grand balls in Stockholm.

Some hours had passed pleasantly and quickly by, when Olga heard the sound of her brother's return. Laying down her book, she rose to meet him, and give him a kind sister's welcome home. But as he entered the room, she exclaimed, " Dear Frederic! are you ill? something is the matter; tell me, dear brother, what it is."

"Do not alarm yourself, Olga dear; I am very well; something has happened.

O sister! how glad I am you were not at this terrible ball!"

"What is it, Fred?" said Olga, endeavoring to be calm.

"Well, you must hear of it sooner or latter; the king has been shot."

"The king shot! O, brother! is he alive?"

"He is, and hopes are entertained that the wound may not prove mortal."

"What a dreadful thing!" said Olga, "When did it happen?"

"This evening, in the ball-room. The assassin has for the present escaped."

"O, who could be so wicked? what could his motive be? Is no one suspected?"

"Many have their suspicions. I have just been told that King Gustavus this day received an anonymous letter, warning him of his immediate danger from a plot that was laid to take away his life, requesting him to remain at home, and avoid balls for a year, and assuring him, that if he went to the masquerade for which he was preparing, he would be assassinated this very night."

"And did he not take warning?"

"No; he read the note with contempt, and entered the ball-room at a late hour. After some time, he observed to a noble near him, 'that he was not deceived in his contempt for the letter, since, had there been any design against his life, no time could be more favorable than that moment.' Without apprehension he then mingled with the crowd, and was preparing to retire from the company, when several persons in masks surrounded him, and at the same instant the king received a shot in the back. You may imagine the scene of confusion which followed! Amid the general tumult and alarm and exclamations of horror, several ladies fainted. No one, however, was allowed to leave the room; the doors were immediately closed and guarded, and a general order given for all the company to unmask. The conspirators must have retired to different parts of the room; I myself picked up pistols and a dagger close to the wounded king."

"And the assassin was not discovered?"

"No person could be detected as the perpetrator of the dreadful deed, though, as I told you, many have their suspicions."

"And the king?"

"He was conveyed to the palace, and the surgeons have extracted a ball and some slugs; they give favorable hopes, but all who love their sovereign feel very apprehensive about him."

"And do not all Swedes love their king, Fred?"

"Alas, Olga, there is a discontented party among the nobles. They have long opposed the measures of the court; they have declared that Gustavus was aiming at despotic power, and on them our suspicions rest."

"Do you think he has aimed at despotic power?"

"He has endeavored to increase his power since the day of the revolution, but unquestionably he has labored to promote the general good of his subjects. Gustavus the Third is a memorable example of a king uniting with the people to oppose the encroachments of a powerful nobility."

"O Frederic! I hope he will recover."

"I hope he will indeed. I am going to the palace now, and trust in the morning to bring you a good report. Good night, dear Olga, I am very thankful you were not at the ball."

In the morning the king was pronounced better, in answer to the numerous inquiries made at the palace. Every exertion was immediately made to discover the murderer. Colonel Cederstrom was very active in taking measures for this purpose. He traced the anonymous letter to a major in the guards, who was apprehended. An order was issued to all the gunsmiths and cutlers in Stockholm, desiring them to give every information in their power concerning the weapons which had been found in the ball-room. A gunsmith who had repaired the pistols, readily recognized them to be the same which he had sent to a nobleman of the name of Ankerstrœm; and the cutler who had made the dagger, referred at once to the same person. In consequence, Ankerstrœm was immediately arrested.

King Gustavus languished twelve days, and then expired. For the first few days the reports of the medical attendants were favorable, but mortification ensued, which terminated his existence. On opening his body, a square piece of lead and two rusty nails were found unextracted within the ribs.

The shocking murder of their king filled all loyal Swedes with grief and consternation. This was increased by the conduct of Gustavus on his death-bed. He displayed throughout his illness that unshaken courage and fortitude which he had manifested on every occasion during his life. But what touched his people still more was his forgiving spirit. Though he was aware that some of his own nobles were the conspirators against his life, and had appointed Ankerstrœm to execute their wicked purpose,—though he remembered with what haughtiness they had opposed him for years, and thrown obstacles in his way,—yet his last words were a declaration of pardon to them. The actual murderer and all he freely forgave.

"Surely your majesty will not pardon Ankerstrœm?" said the Duke of Sudermania, the king's brother; "it would be wrong, in my opinion, to do so. You have shown wondrous clemency in forgiving the conspirators, but with the murderer, Ankerstrœm, justice should take its course."

Those who surrounded the king in his dying moments expressed the same opinion, and earnestly prayed the monarch to retract his pardon.

"If you all think it right and just, be it so," said the expiring king, "but I forgive, as I hope to be forgiven."

Gustavus the Third died, and his son, aged fourteen, was immediately proclaimed king, under the title of Gustavus the Fourth; the Duke of Sudermania being appointed regent, till he should have attained the age of eighteen.

The regicide Ankerstrœm, when he was apprehended, had exclaimed with a triumphant air, "Yes! I am he who has endeavored to deliver his country from a monster and a tyrant!" It was thought he was not alone in his guilt, and suspicions fell on several of the nobility, who were arrested. These suspicions were confirmed by the confession of Ankerstrœm. He said these nobles had appointed him to be the murderer of their sovereign. They received different degrees of punishment, and Ankerstrœm was put to death.

Frederic Cederstrom and his sister were deeply shocked and grieved by the sad event which had taken place. They loved their king, with all his faults, and lamented that the ambition of the nobles should have led them into the perpetration of so fearful a crime. To dissipate their gloomy reflections, Frederic proposed to his sister a change of scene. "Let us leave Stockholm for a time, Olga," he said, "and visit other countries; it will benefit us both."

"Most willingly shall I do so, Frederic," replied Olga. "There is one country I very much wish to visit; and that is England. Suppose we go there?"

"Yes, Olga, we will go to that land of liberty; we shall learn much from a sojourn there."

To England they went, and during a

stay of some months there knew not which to admire most, the affection of the people for their king—George the Third—or the care of the king for his people. The integrity of the institutions, the soundness of the laws, and the personal liberty and freedom of each subject, from the highest to the lowest, all won their admiration. They witnessed with surprise the superior comforts of the peasantry to those of Sweden, and their hearts rejoiced to see the kind beneficence of the noble and the great. Each cared for each; there was not one law for the rich, and another for the poor; none could tyrannize over his fellow man. They admired the schools, charitable institutions, and, above all, the churches and Protestant religion. And when they saw the public acknowledgment of God's hand in all national affairs, and the regard paid to his holy day throughout the land, they wondered not that England was rich and prosperous.

YOUNG LINNÆUS'S EARLY LESSONS IN BOTANY.

See page 202.

Perseverance.

Most little boys and girls are fond of flowers, and those who have gardens of their own, generally spend many happy hours in them, sowing the seeds, watering the young plants, pulling up the weeds, and trimming the borders. To those who, from living in a town, have not this source of enjoyment, how delightful is a walk in the country? roaming through the meadows, gathering the cowslips and primroses, or bounding through the shady wood, full of glee, yet stopping almost every minute to pluck the graceful hare-bell, to admire the beautiful and exquisitely delicate moss, or to search in its hiding place for the modest and fragrant violet. I doubt not, many of you, dear children, have frequently enjoyed such a walk, and I hope that when your admiration has been called forth by the delicate beauty of one flower, or the sweet perfume of another, you have sometimes thought of the great and good God who made them all, and have learned a lesson of his love, and skill, and wisdom, while contemplating these beautiful works of his hands.

Every child loves a daisy, that simple little flower, the harbinger of spring. Did you ever examine it, or think of the wondrous skill of its Maker? If you have not, suppose you learn the following pretty lines:—

> "Not worlds on worlds in phalanx deep
> Need we to prove that God is here,
> The daisy, fresh from winter's sleep,
> Tells of his hand, in lines as clear.
> For who but he, who arch'd the skies,
> And pours the day-spring's living flood,
> Wondrous alike in all he tries,
> Could form the daisy's purple bud?
> Mold its green cup and wiry stem,
> And cut its gold-embossed gem,
> And fling it unrestrain'd and free,
> O'er hill, and dale, and desert sod,
> That man, where'er he walks, may see
> In every step, the stamp of God!"

Now, perhaps, some of you have elder sisters or brothers who study botany. The science of botany arranges plants in their proper classes, and describes their different parts and uses. It is a very interesting and useful science, as by it we learn the nature of plants, and discover which are poisonous, and which are beneficial to man. I am going to tell you a story of the celebrated Swedish botanist who first accurately arranged vegetable productions in classes, and who taught people a great deal about them which they did not know before. His discoveries and his writings have immortalized the name of Carl Linnæus.

It is a story on *perseverance*. Have you this excellent quality, dear child? When you have a task to perform, do you steadily persevere in it till you have overcome every difficulty, or do you soon give it up, saying, "I shall never do this!" or, "I never can learn that! so it is of no use to try." If the latter be the case, attend to this true story. Remember, perseverance can do great things,—it is a mighty conqueror of difficulties. "*But the slothful man saith, There is a lion in the way.*"

In the small hamlet of Rashult, in the province of Smaland, in Sweden, there once lived a poor but worthy clergyman.

He had one little boy, named Carl. The cottage in which they resided was situated on the banks of a beautiful lake, and surrounded by hills, valleys, woods, and fields. Immediately round the cottage was a garden, in which the clergyman, whose name was Nicholas Linnæus, took great delight. He would pass whole hours in it, and a very pretty, well-arranged garden it was, full of Swedish plants and flowers, with many foreign ones besides. Little Carl was very fond of the garden also; from a very early age he was almost constantly in it. His father used to teach him the names of the flowers when he was only three or four years of age, and point out to him the beauty of their color and form in a manner quite interesting to the little boy. Sometimes he would, after showing him a particular kind of plant, send him to seek for another like it; sometimes he would teach him how to transplant, and sometimes he would let him sow the seeds. Then, as he grew older, he would take him into the woods, and tell him the names of the different trees and mosses; he would make him observe how some plants liked water, some heat, and some shade. Insensibly, little Carl inbibed a strong taste for natural history. He loved his garden, and one of the favorite flowers in it was the daisy, which closes every night, and at the approach of rain; but opens its golden eye to the rising sun, from whence it has its name, *day's eye*. The daisies in Sweden are remarkably fine, as indeed are the wild flowers of that country. This hardy little plant, such a favorite with the children in England, appears in the meadows of Sweden directly the snow has left the ground. It holds up its bold little head to welcome the returning sun and warmth, after the long, long sleep of winter; and gladdens the Swedish children as it does those in England.

The purple heath is found on the moors, and the lily sheds its perfume in the valley;—

"But this bold flow'ret climbs the hill,
Hides in the forest, haunts the glen,
Plays on the margin of the rill,
Peeps round the fox's den,

"Within the garden's cultured round
It shares the sweet carnation's bed,
And blooms on consecrated ground
  In honor of the dead.

"The lambkin crops its crimson gem,
The wild-bee murmurs on its breast,
The blue-fly bends its pensile stem
  Light o'er the sky-lark's nest.

"'Tis Flora's page:—in every place,
In every season, fresh and fair,
It opens with perennial grace,
  And blossoms everywhere."

When Carl Linnæus was about six years old, his father, who had some acquaintance with botany, resolved to give him some instruction in it. Accordingly he began to teach him the Latin names for the flowers and plants around him; but these Carl found it very difficult to remember. The lesson was badly learned, and badly said, and at last, the clergyman found it necessary to desire that his little son should not go into the garden till the appointed task was well performed. This was a sad privation to Carl, and like some other little boys, instead of setting manfully to work to learn the difficult lesson, he began to cry, and to say he should never know it. It was not till the evening that the task was accomplished. The next day he had the same number of names given him to get by heart, and again his tears flowed at the thoughts of it.

"I shall never learn these tiresome names," he said, with a deep sigh, as he sat down with the book in his hand.

"Say not so, Carl," replied his father; "you learned the same number of names yesterday."

"But, papa, these Latin words are so very difficult to remember: I am sure I shall never learn them."

"I know they are difficult, but not too difficult for you to learn. Remember, Carl, the lesson requires both patience and perseverance."

"Papa," said the little boy, "may I go and play in the garden first, and learn my lesson when I come in?"

"No, Carl; you may not. The task must be performed first. Now, be a brave boy, and conquer the difficulty. I am going a long walk through the forest this morning, and I shall be glad of your company when you are ready."

"I know I shall never be ready with this tiresome lesson," said Carl despondingly; then as he looked out on the calm lake, and the blue sky, and the tall, dark green pines, he thought how delightful a walk through the forest would be. Turning his eyes then on the lesson in his hand, he again sighed as he contemplated the long names. As he was saying, "No, it is of no use, I *cannot* learn them," his tearful glance fell on the lesson of the day before. "Well, I did get through that," said the little boy, "and it was very difficult; why should I not get through this also? I will try to do so, at all events."

He set to work in earnest, and in the course of an hour said his lesson perfectly. How delightful was the walk through the forest after that! But the following day the lesson seemed as difficult as ever. After looking at it for a little time, Carl resolved to try if he could not persuade his papa to let him give it up altogether. So, going up to him, he said, "Papa, you see the difficulty I have in learning these hard Latin names, may I not give it up till I am older?"

"Certainly not, Carl; persevere, and the lesson will become easier to you every day."

"But I do not see any use in it, papa."

"And I do, my son. If it were useful in no other way, it would be in this, that it teaches you to apply and to persevere. But knowledge, dear Carl, is always useful; and uninteresting as these Latin names may now appear to you, take my word for it, you will live to be thankful that you ever learned them. In some way or other, you will find the knowledge useful."

"I love flowers," said little Carl, "but I cannot endure these difficult names for them."

"If you love flowers, my son, would you not like to know all you can about them? There is, I feel sure, much, very much yet to be discovered concerning plants. We know a little, and that only makes us wish to know more. A wide and interesting field is open to those who desire to study botany, or natural history in any of its branches."

"Is natural history amusing, papa?"

"It is so attractive, Carl, that those who once engage in it seldom give it up. The naturalist meets with endless variety, and at every step discovers in the works of nature beautiful contrivances which escape the eye of a common observer."

"I should like to be a naturalist, papa," said little Carl; "what kinds of things do they discover?"

"They see that plants and shrubs are small in cold countries, and large in hot ones. They have found in the East a plant with leaves more than six yards in breadth, shaped like an umbrella; and in South America there is one with flowers of such great size, that the children wear them in play, as hats."

"O! I should like to see that plant."

"In the warm countries the flowers are very large and beautiful, and the trees grow to a great height. But how we must admire our own forest trees. Look at the graceful, silvery birch! and then think how useful it is to us. We roof our houses and huts with its bark, while our fishermen make shoes of it; then with the inner bark we tan leather, and make a cement for mending broken china. The Laplanders fasten large pieces of it together as an outer garment to keep off the rain; the Kamschatdales make hats and cups of it, and the people in North America, canoes and dishes. Ground, and mixed with meal, it is in Norway used as food for pigs. And in Russia an essential oil is extracted from it, which gives a peculiar scent to Russia leather."

"O, papa, how useful it is! pray tell me something else."

"Not now, Carl; you have your lesson to learn. As I intend you to enter the Church, it is quite necessary you should know something of the nature of herbs and plants, in order that if you should have charge of a parish in a wild and remote part of the country, you may not be ignorant of the simple remedies which the poor people may require, when, if the doctor lives at a distance, they look to the clergyman for help and advice. Now, my boy, attend to your lesson."

But Carl did not feel inclined to attend. He sat with his book in his hand, not even trying to learn: and it was not till the evening that the lesson was said. Then the clergyman, taking his little boy by the hand, led him into the garden. "See, my son," he said, as they stopped before the little plot of ground which belonged to Carl, "see how your garden is neglected! It is now three days since you have given it any attention, and you see the consequences. Look at the numerous weeds which have sprung up even in that short time!"

"Ah, papa," said Carl, "I will set to work at once, and pull up all the weeds, and water the flowers, and make my garden look quite nice again."

"And will you persevere till every weed is rooted up?"

"Certainly, papa; I do not like weeds."

"Neither do I, Carl; and therefore I intend to persevere with *you*. It will be my endeavor to pull up that hurtful and wide-spreading weed of *idleness*, and to water and encourage the little plant of perseverance. Your heart, my child, is like a garden; if neglected, the weeds will abundantly spring up in it, and I shall see few pleasant flowers. But I must try, and you must try, that this be not the case. You want perseverance, Carl. You have a little, for you can evince it in your garden; but you must have more. You must persevere at your lessons also. You must get rid of that bad habit of saying, 'I cannot do this,' and 'I shall never do that.' Nothing great or good was ever yet done without perseverance. Try to conquer difficulties. Why, the little birds you are so fond of, give you a lesson on it. Look at the patient perseverance they display in building their nests! and if by some accident one is destroyed, how quickly they set to work to build another! Imitate them, my dear boy. You know not how much of your success in life may depend on that little word *try*."

Carl thought of what his father had said to him, and wisely determined to try and

conquer the difficulties of his Latin lesson.
It was hard work sometimes; he had to
learn the long names over and over again,
before he could say them well. But he
did not give up; he tried on, and he
found his task easier every day. He soon
could learn it quickly, and you may be
astonished when I tell you, that at last it
became quite a pleasure to him.

Now little Carl Linnæus had learned
two things. He had learned to persevere,
and he had learned to remember names,
and these two things became of infinite
service to him in after life. From this
time his perseverance was striking, and
his mind took a decided turn for nomen-
clature or names.

I will tell you a few of the difficulties
this eminent Swedish naturalist had to
contend with, before he attained such
high honor in his native country as
to be styled "the Father of Natural
History."

Linnæus, when young, paid much attention to the habits and distinctions of birds
and insects, as well as to the nature and

properties of plants, and when he was about twenty, he first formed that fixed determination of devoting himself to the study of natural history which neither poverty nor misery was able afterward to shake.

He had received some education to prepare him for the medical profession, which he preferred to that of the Church. Being at home for a vacation, he told his father of the great desire he had to understand botany, and of the books he had read on the subject.

"Now it is my earnest wish," he continued, "to prosecute my studies at the university of Upsal; can you send me there, father?"

"My dear son," replied the clergyman, "I should much wish to do so, but my income, as you know, is a very small one; the utmost I could allow you would be forty dollars a year, and how could you live on that in Upsal?"

Linnæus was silent for some minutes, and then he said, "It is a small sum indeed with which to meet the expenses of a university education; but father, I have courage and perseverance, thanks to you, and I will venture."

It was truly a miserable stipend on which to depend, and nothing less than the most biting poverty could be the result of such a measure; but Linnæus was not dismayed. He did not say, "I never can live on this," but, "I will try what I can do."

He tried; but so great was his destitution while doing so, that he often did not know how to find a meal. His clothes became very shabby, and he had to mend his shoes with folds of brown paper. Hungry and cold, and in want of the necessaries of life, he in vain endeavored to increase his scanty income by private pupils. No help could be obtained from home, and it is difficult to conceive how such a youth could struggle against the adversity, or bear up under the privations which oppressed him. But he did, well and manfully. And notwithstanding his poverty, he diligently persevered in attendance upon the courses of lectures connected with his future profession; so eager was his desire for knowledge, hunger itself could not abate it.

His diligence was at length rewarded by his obtaining a scholarship, which slightly increased his income, and soon afterward, having attracted the notice of some of the professors by his persevering industry, they procured him private pupils. The clouds began to disperse. Finding him to be a clever young man, and well acquainted with natural history, the professor of divinity requested his assistance in preparing a work illustrating the plants mentioned in Holy Scripture; while the professor of botany appointed him his deputy lecturer, took him into his house as tutor to his children, and gave him free access to a fine library and collection of drawings.

How pleased was Linnæus now? But was he idle, now that he was relieved from poverty? No; with the same indefatigable industry and perseverance which characterized him all his life, in addition to the duties to which he had to attend, he began to write some of his celebrated works on botany. And now he found the benefit of having learned the names of plants when young; now he was very glad that his father had made him conquer the difficulty which he at first thought so great.

After some time, during which he had been diligently acquiring knowledge, Linnæus proceeded, at the expense of the university of Upsal, on his celebrated journey into Lapland. On horseback and on foot, alone and slenderly provided, he traveled upward of four thousand miles. Here again no difficulties daunted him; he persevered through all the obstacles he met with in that wild and dreary journey, and succeeded in what he had undertaken to do.

Many were the interesting observations Linnæus made in his Lapland tour. At Tornea, he was told of a disease among the cattle, which killed a great many of them in the winter, but was still more prevalent in the spring, when they were first turned out to grass, a circumstance for which the inhabitants could not account. Linnæus examined the place where the cattle had fed, and found it to be a marsh in which the plant called cow-bane grew in abundance. He pointed it out to the people, and they were thus able to guard against the danger ever after.

The botanist knew the effect of light on plants, and that when deprived of it, they become white and colorless. He had observed how beneficial the influence of light is to trees, by seeing that their branches were generally thicker and more full of leaves on the side exposed to the sun, than on the opposite one. And he saw that this knowledge was useful to the Laplanders.

They are unacquainted with the compass, and often would they lose their way in their long journeys through wild regions without roads or paths, were they not guided by various natural appearances, which enable them to distinguish the points of north and south. In Lapland Linnæus saw that useful plant, the rein-deer moss. It is the food of the valuable **rein-deer**, that animal so prized by the Laplanders. The moss is of a whitish color, and grows to the height of at least a foot, covering the ground like snow.

The poor Laplanders derive several of their comforts from the mosses. They make excellent beds of that species called the golden maiden-hair, by cutting thick layers of it, one of which serves as a mattress, the other as a coverlet. Linnæus used such a bed; he found the mossy cushions very elastic, and he could roll them up and carry them under his arm during the day, without any inconvenience. If after long use the moss became hard, its elasticity and freshness were soon restored by dipping it into water. The little babies were wrapped in it, without any other clothing, and it lined the inside of their leathern cradles, so that they had soft and warm nests in that cold country. This kind of moss is called bog-moss; it is particularly soft, like a thick fur. You see the provision which a merciful God makes for all the wants of his creatures. "The earth is full of the goodness of the Lord."

This was a long and desolate journey for young Linnæus to take alone. Children in England have no idea of the bitter cold of those northern regions, where the sun for months together is below the horizon. Yet the Laplander loves his home. Had you met the botanist on his return from his dreary journey, you might have asked him,—

> "With blue cold nose and wrinkled brow
> Traveler, whence comest thou?"

And his answer would have been—

> "From Lapland woods and hills of frost,
> By the rapid rein-deer cross'd;
> Where tapering grows the gloomy fir,
>   And the stunted juniper;
> Where the wild hare and the crow
> Whiten in surrounding snow;
> Where the shivering huntsmen tear
> His fur coat from the grim white bear;
> Where the wolf and arctic fox
> Prowl among the lonely rocks;
> And tardy suns to deserts drear,
> Give days and nights of half a year.
> From icy oceans, where the whale
> Tosses in foam his lashing tail;
> Where the snorting sea-horse shows
> His ivory teeth in grinning rows;

> Where, tumbling in their sealskin boat,
> Fearless the hungry fishers float;
> And from the teeming seas supply
> The food those niggard plains deny."

Linnæus returned from his Lapland tour with a fresh stock of knowledge, and an increased love for natural history. But he was still poor. When he wished to take his degree as doctor of medicine, all the money he could possibly scrape together for the purpose amounted only to $75. With this sum, he set out on his travels in search of a university where he might obtain his degree in the cheapest manner. He found one in Holland, and there he also found plenty of employment in arranging the beautiful garden, museum, and library, of a wealthy Dutch banker. While thus employed, he also, with wonderful energy and industry, wrote and published many works. The immense quantity of business he got through, and the labor he bestowed on it, was quite astonishing; but the once idle little Carl could now make prodigious efforts in overcoming difficulties. Indeed, he seems to have possessed powers of application quite beyond those of ordinary men. Day and night he worked at his favorite pursuits; indefatigable and persevering, he never knew an idle moment.

About this time he visited England, and having been liberally remunerated by his friend, the Dutch banker, was able in that country to make a considerable addition to his collection of plants and books.

It was when walking one day on a common near London that Linnæus first saw the furze. He was so much delighted with the golden bloom of this beautiful shrub, that uttering an exclamation of surprise and admiration, he fell down on his knees to admire it. He tried to preserve some plants of it through the winter in Sweden, under cover, with as much care as we bestow on hot-house plants, but without success. It will not live in a northern clime.

On his return to Sweden, the prospects of Linnæus began to brighten. He commenced practice in Stockholm as a physician, and received a pension of two hundred ducats from government on condition that he should give public lectures in mineralogy and botany. His botanical fame spread over all Europe, and his superior knowledge in natural history was universally admitted. His works were read and admired. Those on botany are particularly famed for his system of names;—a system by which every known plant can be spoken of in two Latin words. He wrote an extraordinary number of works on various branches of natural history. When about to publish one of the most celebrated of them, he examined the characters of no less than eight thousand flowers!

Always industrious, and ever seeking to acquire fresh knowledge, Linnæus made many discoveries in his favorite pursuit. A friend once gave him some seeds of a plant, which, having sown in his greenhouse, they soon produced two beautiful flowers. When Linnæus first saw them, the gardener was absent, and in the evening when he took him, with a lantern, to see them, they were nowhere to be found. Linnæus concluded they had been destroyed by insects, but on visiting his greenhouse next morning, there were the flowers, looking as fresh as ever. Accordingly he took his gardener again in the evening to see and admire them; but again they had disappeared! To the great surprise of Linnæus, he saw them the next morning, when he rose early to visit his green-house, just in the place where he had seen them the day before, and blooming brightly. Calling the gardener—for he thought he had better see these mysterious flowers while he could— the botanist expressed his astonishment.

"Ah, sir," said the gardener, "these flowers cannot be the same you saw yesterday; these must have blown to-day."

The man was satisfied this was the case: but Linnæus was not. As soon as it was dark, he once more visited the plant, and after lifting up all the leaves, one by one, he found the two flowers folded up, and so closely concealed under them, that it was impossible, at first sight, to discover where they were. This led him to direct his attention to other plants of the same tribe, and he found to his delight and satisfaction that all their flowers possessed the property, in a greater or less degree, of closing at night; and this he called "the sleep of plants."

There are many wonderful and curious things, dear children, to be learned from the study of natural history. Have you ever heard of the plant in the East, which is called, "the flower of the air." It is found in abundance near the river Ganges, and it grows and even blossoms in the air, when hung up, without attaching itself to any solid body. The smell of the flower is most delightful, and the inhabitants frequently suspend it from the ceilings of their rooms, where it will vegetate for years. Or have you read of the extraordinary flower discovered by a naturalist in the Island of Sumatra, which measured a yard across? the petals being twelve inches in length, and the nectary capable of holding twelve pints of water! Did you know that in Sweden and Norway the poor people make cakes of the inner bark of the pine-tree, mixed with a small portion of flour? The children in those countries are **very** fond of the fresh bark, when ground into powder. In Norway, too, they make bread of barley and oatmeal, which will keep thirty or forty years; and at a christening feast, bread is sometimes eaten which was made in the time of the child's great-grandfather.

But to return to Linnæus. From this time his life was one of increasing fame and prosperity. Books and collections were sent to him from all parts of the world, and his pupils communicated to him the result of their travels in Europe, Asia, Africa, and America. He was named professor of medicine and professor of botany in the university where he had studied as a poor, half-starved youth. He was enabled to purchase estates worth 80,000 Swedish dollars; and was at length raised to the nobility, receiving the title of Von Linné. Such was the result of his perseverance in study, and steady constant industry and application!

Linnæus died in the 71st year of his age. He was buried in the Cathedral of Upsal, the whole university attending his funeral, and his pall being borne by sixteen doctors of physic, all of whom had been his pupils.

A general mourning took place on the occasion at Upsal; and King Gustavus the Third not only caused a medal to be struck expressive of the public loss, but introduced the subject in a speech from the throne, regarding the death of Linnæus as a national calamity.

Children! when you have difficulties to overcome, think of Carl Linnæus: and imitate his industry, his energy, and his perseverance.

YOUNG ERIC DECLARED KING.

See page 230

The Three Pictures.

HERE are three pictures: can you explain them?

Round the great Mora Stone, near Upsal, a place consecrated by ancient recollections, there stands a vast assembly. It is in the year 1396. Something of great importance seems to absorb universal attention. The looks of all present, warriors, clergy, nobles, and peasants, are eagerly bent on two figures in the center of this great crowd, standing near the stone. One is that of a stately, queen-like woman, attired in regal magnificence, and wearing a crown on her head. She looks proudly round on the vast multitude, but there is kindness as well as pride in the glance.

The other is that of a little boy, whom she holds by the hand, and gazes upon, from time to time, with a look of tenderness and love. He is a fine-looking child. His long fair hair floats over his shoulders,

as he stands there with head uncovered;
and his eyes glisten with pleasure and animation at a scene so new to him. And
now the nobles and warriors press forward,
and, one by one, laying their hands on the
Mora Stone, vow fealty to young Eric as
the successor to their queen. The child
—he is but five years old—looks on with
wonder and curiosity, and grasps more
firmly the hand of his stately aunt.

He sees himself to be the object of great
attention, he sees the searching glances of
the Swedish warriors fixed upon him, he
hears himself declared king of Norway,
Sweden, and Denmark, even during the
lifetime of his royal aunt, and he wonders
what it all means. Occasionally, he lifts
his inquiring eyes to the lady's countenance; but she is watching the proceedings
with a calm and pleased expression. So
Eric knows all must be right, and again
turns to admire the glittering swords, and
nodding plumes, and waving banners.

Who was this queen? She was a woman
of great ambition, but of remarkable pru-

dence. She was one, who by the powers of her mind alone, for armies she had none, triumphed over every obstacle, and caused herself to be elected sovereign of Norway, Sweden, and Denmark. Yet each of these kingdoms had an insuperable objection to be governed by a woman. They deemed it dishonorable, and therefore, at Mora Stone, they declared her nephew, Eric, not only her successor but her colleague. They knew he would have nothing to do with the government, but they did not like it to be said, that the warlike descendants of the fierce Northmen were ruled by a woman. But she ruled them well. The coolness with which she formed her designs, the steadiness with which she put them into execution, and the peace and prosperity which accompanied her and her people through life, are the best monuments of her greatness. Few reigns have been more remarkable than hers.

She was the celebrated Queen Margaret, who, by the union of Calmar, made Norway, Sweden, and Denmark, subject to the same scepter, though each realm continued to be governed by its own laws.

The next picture is one in Switzerland.

From a good-sized cottage situated in one of her beautiful valleys, there issues forth a family party. All seem delighted with the grandeur and loveliness of the scene around them. The magnificent and snow-capped mountains rising into the clouds, the smiling fertile valley, dotted with its pretty cottages, the sparkling rivulet, the lake in the distance, all claim their admiration. While the children run to gather the wild flowers scattered in rich profusion around, the father seats himself on a mossy bank, leans his head upon his hand, and enjoys the scene. As he gazes, his thoughts revert to his own country, and to his own home, which is far, far away. He looks thoughtful, but not unhappy, though his home is in Sweden, and he will never more see his fatherland.

"Is Count Gottorp pleased with our beautiful country?" says a Swiss peasant to an old servant in the cottage, as they are preparing the evening meal, which, to please the children, is to be arranged in the pretty garden.

"Yes, he is much pleased with it," answered old Sigismund, "he says it reminds him of Sweden."

"It must be a great change for him," observes the peasant.

"Of course it is, my friend. Sweden is much colder than your country."

"Ah, he feels a greater change than the change of climate. Sigismund, it is of no use concealing it from me; your master has been a great man in Sweden, and his real name is not Count Gottorp."

"And how did you discover that, friend?"

"I have heard the children talking, and I have eyes too, Master Sigismund. I see many things, and among others, that you have not been accustomed to do such work as you do now. You have had servants to wait on you formerly, or I am much mistaken."

"Well, Pierre," Sigismund replies, "as

you are now engaged in this establishment, I will treat you with confidence, and tell you a secret,—but mind, it is a great secret. My master's real name is not Count Gottorp."

"Ah, but that I knew before," replies Pierre, rather disappointed. "What was his rank in Sweden, Sigismund?"

"Well, as you know so much, I may as well tell you a little more," says the old servant, perhaps a little proud of letting the simple peasant know the dignity of his master's former station. "Count Gottorp, Pierre, is no less a person than the king of Sweden."

"The king of Sweden! O, Sigismund!"

"Yes; that is, he is not exactly the king now, because he has abdicated the throne, but he *was* the king, and that is almost the same thing."

"Well, now, I should think it very different. But why did he abdicate?"

"Why, they said he did not govern well. The nobles complained, the burghers complained, and the peasants complained. So they desired their sovereign to abdicate, and he did. For my own part, I think he is happier since he gave up the cares of royalty; he had a troublesome reign, and he appears to me much more gentle and calm and amiable in these peaceful valleys, than he was when seated on the throne of Sweden, with such numerous things to disturb and perplex him."

"What did he to displease his subjects?"

"Many extraordinary things, they say. The revolution, however, was effected without bloodshed, and my royal master was arrested in his own palace."

"He seems to entertain a great dislike to the French emperor, Napoleon."

"He does indeed! He never would have anything to say to him, and always calls him 'Monsieur Napoleon Buonaparte.' I remember his sending back some noble order the king of Prussia had given him, because he had conferred the same order on the Emperor Napoleon. Between you and me, Pierre, I believe my royal master has a little obstinacy in his disposition, like his great ancestor, Charles the Twelfth. He quarreled with France, Russia, Denmark, Prussia, and England, and then with his own subjects. So I think he is happier without a kingdom than with one. But now let us spread the table, Pierre. The royal children never had such a treat as this in Stockholm."

This exiled monarch was Gustavus Adolphus the Fourth, son of the king who was assassinated at the masqued ball.

The third picture is that of a general officer entering the city of Stockholm. The citizens have all put on their holiday attire, and crowd the streets with smiling faces, to welcome the stranger. He rides on a beautiful horse, attended by some officers, and courteously returns the greetings of the people.

"This is our new crown prince, Charles John," they exclaim one to another; "he is a brave general, and a good statesman. I hope he will make a good king."

The children ask who the brave soldier is.

"He is one of Napoleon's most celebrated generals," is the reply, "and is just elected our crown prince."

"But why is the throne of our great Gustavus Adolphus to be given to a stranger and a Frenchman?" asks the son of a Swedish noble.

"Because it is thought he is the fittest person to have it," replies his father, "and because our present king has no child. He is well known to many of our Swedish families from his kindness to Swedish prisoners. You may think it strange, my son, that this very man, whom we now regard as our future king, is the son of a petty lawyer at Pau, and commenced his military career as a private in the marines."

The general, whose fortunes were so remarkable, was Bernadotte. He was crowned king of Sweden and Norway, under the title of Charles the Fourteenth, and after a wise and good reign, was succeeded in 1844 by his son, the present king, Oscar the First.

Bernadotte had seen enough of the miseries of war, to declare, when seated on the throne, that "Peace is the only glorious object of a wise and enlightened government."

THE END.